FOUL DEEDS & SUSPICIOUS
DEATHS IN COVENTRY

FOUL DEEDS AND SUSPICIOUS DEATHS Series

Foul Deeds and Suspicious Deaths series explores in detail crimes of passion, brutal murders, grisly deeds and foul misdemeanours. From Victorian street crime, to more modern murder where passion, jealousy, or social deprivation brought unexpected violence to those involved. From mysterious death to murder and manslaughter, the books are a fascinating insight into not only those whose lives are forever captured by the suffering they endured, but also into the society that moulded and shaped their lives. Each book takes you on a journey into the darker and unknown side of the area.

Other titles in the series

Foul Deeds and Suspicious Deaths in Blackburn & Hyndburn, Steve Greenhalgh
ISBN: 1-903425-18-2. £9.99

Foul Deeds and Suspicious Deaths in and around Chesterfield, Geoffrey Sadler
ISBN: 1-903425-30-1. £9.99

More Foul Deeds and Suspicious Deaths in and around Chesterfield, Geoffrey Sadler
ISBN: 1-903425-68-9. £9.99

Foul Deeds and Suspicious Deaths in & around Durham, Maureen Anderson
ISBN: 1-903425-46-8. £9.99

Foul Deeds and Suspicious Deaths in and around Halifax, Stephen Wade
ISBN: 1-903425-45-X. £9.99

Foul Deeds and Suspicious Deaths in Leeds, David Goodman
ISBN: 1-903425-08-5. £9.99

Foul Deeds and Suspicious Deaths in Manchester, Martin Baggoley
ISBN: 1-903425-65-4. £9.99

Foul Deeds and Suspicious Deaths in Newcastle, Maureen Anderson
ISBN: 1-903425-34-4. £9.99

Foul Deeds and Suspicious Deaths in Nottingham, Kevin Turton
ISBN: 1-903425-35-2. £9.99

Foul Deeds and Suspicious Deaths around Pontefract and Castleford, Keith Henson
ISBN: 1-903425-54-9. £ 9.99

Foul Deeds and Suspicious Deaths in and around Rotherham, Kevin Turton
ISBN: 1-903425-27-1. £9.99

Foul Deeds and Suspicious Deaths Around the Tees, Maureen Anderson
ISBN: 1-903425-26-3. £9.99

More Foul Deeds and Suspicious Deaths in Wakefield, Kate Taylor
ISBN: 1-903425-48-4. £9.99

Foul Deeds and Suspicious Deaths in York, Keith Henson
ISBN: 1-903425-33-6. £9.99

Foul Deeds and Suspicious Deaths on the Yorkshire Coast, Alan Whitworth
ISBN: 1-903425-01-8. £9.99

Please contact us via any of the methods below for more
information or a catalogue.
WHARNCLIFFE BOOKS
47 Church Street – Barnsley – South Yorkshire – S70 2AS
Tel: 01226 734555 – 734222 Fax: 01226 734438
E-mail: enquiries@pen-and-sword.co.uk –
Website: www.wharncliffebooks.co.uk

Foul Deeds & Suspicious Deaths in
COVENTRY

DAVID McGRORY

Series Editor
Brian Elliott

Wharncliffe Books

First Published in Great Britain in 2004 by
Wharncliffe Books
an imprint of
Pen and Sword Books Ltd.
47 Church Street
Barnsley
South Yorkshire
S70 2AS

Copyright © David McGrory 2004

ISBN: 1-903425-57-3

Typeset in 11/13pt Plantin by Mac Style Ltd, Scarborough.

Printed and bound in England by
CPI UK.

Pen and Sword Books Ltd incorporates the Imprints of
Pen & Sword Aviation, Pen & Sword Maritime,
Pen & Sword Military, Wharncliffe Books,
Pen & Sword Select, Pen and Sword Military Classics
and Leo Cooper.

For a complete list of Pen & Sword titles please contact
PEN & SWORD BOOKS LIMITED
47 Church Street
Barnsley
South Yorkshire
S70 2BR
England
E-mail: enquiries@pen-and-sword.co.uk
Website: www.pen-and-sword.co.uk

Contents

Dedication

I would like to dedicate this work to the victims of the foul deeds in this book. Gerard de Pucelle, Hugh de Balisall, Robert Underwood, Ivor de Tanur, Roger Stirthup, William de Essenby, William de Parber, Alice le Moun, Nicholas de Wroxhalle, William Gophil, Hugh Russell, Richard de Sowe, John Cristleton, William Cristleton, Ralph Giffard, Richard Stafford, Richard Woodville, John Woodville, Thomas Harrington, Henry Mumford, Robert Mallory, Joan Ward, Alice Lansdail, Thomas Lansdail, Hosea Hawkins, Thomas Wrexham, Robert Hockett, Thomas Bond, Robert Silksby, Lawrence Saunders, Robert Glover, John Glover, William Glover, Cornelius Bungay, John Carelesse, Jocelyn Palmer, William Bennet, Adam Tilley, Thomas Edwards, Charles Pinchbeck, John Newbold, William Harris, William Law, Emma Golsby, Eliza Webb, Elizabeth Kington, Charlotte Fawson, Betsy Beamish, Emily Beamish, Harriet Marston, John Millward, Charlotte Taylor, Mary Phillips and Richard Phillips. Also twelve inmates of Bond's Hospital and other unnamed victims.

Acknowledgements

The information for this book comes from a wide variety of sources but I am especially indebted to Andrew Mealy and the staff of Coventry Local Studies, Coventry Libraries, for their continuing support and supplying materials and pictures, and the *Coventry Evening Telegraph* for material and pictures. I also offer thanks to Chris and Frank Barnes, Gordon Cowley, Albert Peck and John Ashby. The illustrations are from the David McGrory Collection unless credited otherwise.

Introduction

When one sets foot into the world of foul deeds little does one know whom he shall meet there, from bishops, priests, mayors, earls and lords to soldiers, weavers, cappers and butchers. Many who committed the deeds described within this volume held a streak of violence within them, others were victims who had problems with their partners, or were simply in the wrong place at the wrong time. Others suffered foul deaths that were sanctioned by the church, suffering as religious martyrs simply at the whim of the pervading religious belief of the time. This book contains many victims, but also describes the time, the passions of life and the details of daily life in earlier centuries that enrich our understanding of Coventry past.

Despite the fact that medieval Coventry was full of dangerous weapons, one of the most popular for murder was a heavy stick, while amongst the nobility the sword did the damage. In the eighteenth century the pistol was the favourite weapon and while the nineteenth century's most frequent methods were arsenic or a sharp 'bright' kitchen knife, which brought with it one of the most common techniques of the time; slitting throats from ear to ear.

Most recorded foul deeds from Coventry's past are remembered here, but not all as space does not permit, or there simply is not enough information. One such crime took place at the *White Lion Inn* in Smithford Street when Thomas Wilday murdered his aunt, Susannah Wale, the landlady and her niece, Ann Shenstone. Wilday was hanged on Whitley Common on the 17 April 1734 and was then gibbeted.

The last public execution took place in the city on Thursday, August 9 1849 when Mary Ball of Nuneaton was hanged before the city gaol wall for murdering her husband by poison. The crime itself took place in Nuneaton so I have not included it in this book.

As for suspicious deaths, such events appear nearly non-existent; for in the past modern thinking about crime and forensic techniques were not available to cast doubt on the huge number of 'accidental' deaths which appeared to be part of daily life. People fell into boiling vats of beer, blew themselves up, poisoned and gassed themselves, fell down stairs or off horses and no one looked too closely, or asked too many questions. Inquests were always held on such episodes, usually in pubs, and juries appeared more than ready to accept easy verdicts. Much of the information in this book comes from such inquests, which, in the nineteenth century at least, went into cases of murder in great detail. This often meant that the actual trials themselves at the assizes were mere formalities.

Justice of a different sort could be found in medieval times; for those who claimed sanctuary, whatever their crime, were protected by the church. Once their crime was confessed to the coroner who attended them in church they had forty days to abjure the realm. Sometimes they did not make it out of the country because they lost their lives, on the way when they were caught by the families of their victims. Justice in the distant past was generally swift and often brutal.

Foul Deeds and Suspicious Deaths in Coventry starts in the twelfth century with the death of Earl Marmion as he tried to take Coventry Castle and cascades through the centuries ending with a lonely suicide on Gibbet Hill in 1922. Those who want more should read my *Swing 'em Fair: Coventry's Darker Side*, published by Jones/Sands Publishing.

CHAPTER 1

Marmion, Nonant, Ribbaud and Others

It appears that the earliest reference to a foul deed in Coventry was in 1143 when Earl Robert Marmion of Tamworth, a man described as being 'great in warre', rode into Coventry with a force of men. Marmion, a supporter of King Stephen entered the city in late August, headed straight for the priory of St Mary and is said to have driven the monks from the building. Once the building was occupied, Marmion constructed fortifications around it, which included the digging of trenches and mantraps. Meanwhile the men of the Earl of Chester, Ranulf Gernon, watched from nearby Coventry Castle but did nothing, perhaps because they were awaiting reinforcements.

As nothing was happening Marmion, known for his arrogance and bravado, took to riding out alone each day, parading his defiance before the castle. This was all very well until one day the earl's men unexpectedly began to pour forth from the castle gate and Marmion in a sudden panic galloped back toward the priory. He did not, however, make it to safety as he came crashing down into one of his own mantraps. There are two accounts of what happened next, one says that he lay in the ditch some hours with a broken leg before being dispatched by a cobbler. Another version, which is probably nearer the truth, is that being injured and unable to escape he was eventually spotted by a common foot soldier who decapitated him. So ended the life of the great Earl Marmion, headless in a Coventry ditch.

Interestingly, Marmion was attacking the castle of an ally, for Ranulf Gernon was also on the side of Stephen. Why did he do it? It seems that Ranulf Gernon had promised to give Coventry to Marmion, but had probably changed his mind. This claim was later put forward again by Marmion's sons. Another interesting fact concerning this event is that in 1938 when the

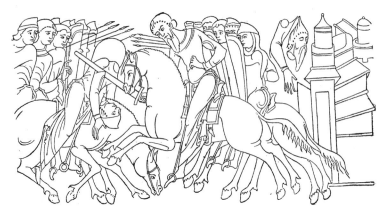

Soldiers of the time of Earl Marmion and the Earl of Chester. Two, like Marmion, had lost their heads!

Blue Coat School was being underpinned, parts of the priory entrance came to light. During the dig a group of skeletons was

A skeleton being unearthed during a Shelton dig in the 1930s. Albert Peck

found, huddled against an old stone wall. Several of the remains showed cuts in their skulls caused by swords. The question is who were these men thrown into a roughly dug pit against an old wall, by the main entrance to the priory? Could they be men who died during the attack, and if that was the case, why after the event were they not given a proper burial? Alternatively, and most likely, it appears that no one knew they were there, and that these men were deliberately hidden. Perhaps Marmion's act of driving the monks from the priory was more violent than was supposed and the consequences were hidden from prying eyes, not to come to light until accidently discovered over 700 years later.

The priory was the scene of other deaths and suspicious incidents. In 1185 Gerard le Pucelle, Bishop of Coventry, died suddenly and was buried in the great Chapter House. Talk after his death suggested poison being the tool of his fate, administered by an unknown hand. He was soon followed by someone who may have been responsible – Hugh de Nonant. Nonant was an advisor to King Richard I; he also held the post of Sheriff of Staffordshire. He acquired the bishopric without election by paying cash to Richard. Consequently the monks disliked him, but not as much as he disliked them, for Nonant was a notorious monk hater. He was once noted as saying, 'If I had my way there would not be a monk left in England. To the devil with all monks.'

One of his first acts was to ignore a papal decree and move his chair to Lichfield, home to secular canons, not monks. From there he changed his title to Bishop of Coventry and Lichfield. His malice quickly bore down on the monks of Coventry as he began to cut down their food supply and illegally took their possessions. He also took power from the Prior, making himself all-powerful.

This led to an event that was described by Richard of Devizes, thus:

On a certain day, when the bishop was superintending the workpeople at Coventry, this monk (from Burton) stood close at his side, with the bishop resting on him familiarly. To whom the bishop said, 'Is it not right and proper, my monk, even in thy judgement, that the great beauty of so fine a church and such a splendid edifice, should rather be appropriated to god's than devils?' And while the monk was considering these words, he went on: 'I call my clerks gods, and my monks devils.' And thereupon wagging his finger on his right hand towards his clerks, who stood about, he continued, 'I say ye are gods, and ye are all children of the Highest.' And then he turned again to the left, and concluded to the monk, 'But ye monks shall perish like devils, and as one and the greatest of your princes ye shall fall away into hell, because ye are devils upon earth. Verily, if I should have to officiate for a dead monk, which I should loathe to do so, I should commend his soul to the devil, not to God.'

As he said these words a block of stone fell from the church tower missing Nonant by inches, but smashing out the brains of the monk beside him. An accident maybe, but what happened next makes one think it deliberate. Soon after this Nonant held a synod at the priory and an argument broke out between him and the monks; this resulted in him being attacked by them before the high altar and being struck on the head with the crucifix.

Nonant petitioned William Longchamps, Richard's regent, for the monks to be expelled from their house, saying, that they had deserted their rule, and charging them with becoming, 'contaminated by secular pollution' and worst for spilling his blood, their bishop's blood, before the high altar. It was decreed that the monks of Coventry Priory be expelled and replaced by canons from Lichfield. Prior Moyses went into exile in Rome and the monks scattered, some begging on the streets for survival. Nonant's power grew and he became a close ally of Prince John, deposing Longchamps and getting John onto the throne. On Richard's return Nonant himself was cast from his seat, he did, however, recover it by paying Richard 5,000 marks in 1194.

Coventry's notorious bishop Nonant died in 1198 and on his deathbed, fearing God's judgement he gathered a group of religious dignitaries and confessed a catalogue of sins. Roger of Wendover wrote:

But the religious men who stood by his bed were puzzled what to do after

An early seal of a bishop of Coventry. Nonant's seal would have been much like this.

Seal of Richard Peche, Bishop of Coventry, A.D. 1161–1182.

INSCRIPTION—

**SIGILLVM. RICARDI .. D...CIA.
COVENTRENSIS. EPISCOPI.**

hearing of such a wicked life ... and they remained silent. ... Then the bishop, in the hearing of all confessed that he had expelled the monks of Coventry, and ... had introduced irreligious priests in their stead. He chose to atone for his sins by dying in the habit of those he had, 'persecuted, and reduced to beggary'.

The first known execution in Coventry was recorded in the chronicle of Robert of Gloucester in the thirteenth century. This is the first account of a man being 'sent to Coventry' for execution, and as Coventry appeared to have been used often for executions it may be the origin of the famous saying, for if one was sent to Coventry in this sense no one would ever talk to them again.

Robert wrote that while Henry III (1216–72) was keeping court at Woodstock a secular priest was found hiding in the king's chamber. He initially made himself out to be slow-witted, but was subsequently discovered to have been engaged to murder the king. Robert tells the story:

The country was ripe for rebellion, but as yet no de Montfort had appeared to check the designs of the King, and little demand had been made for the formation of a Parliament for the adjustment of the public interest and the country's good. A council had been held until late one winter's eve at the Royal Manor of Woodstock, to consider and remedy the growing troubles of the State, but as deepening shadows grew apace the King left the Hall, tired and weary, for the rest of his chamber.

But with his mind filled with anxious cares sleep forsook him, and luckily it was so, for a grating noise, as of someone endeavouring to undo the fastenings of the window aroused him from his reverie; so pulling aside the arras he beheld a tall figure busy unfastening the lattice. Noiselessly he called his attendants from an adjoining room, who, after a struggle, succeeded in effecting a capture, and when the prisoner was brought before the King he said he was a priest named Ribbaud, and was connected with a northern monastery.

He likewise confessed to being hired by conspirators to take the King's life. At his trial he was condemned to be sent to

Coventry; and there, in the presence of the people, to be, 'torne by wild horses, and drawn thro' the streets till life leave bodie,' that is, tied to the tails of two swift horses, drawn along the ground, and dragged to death, which punishment, being duly performed, the lifeless mass, was hung, drawn and quartered, and his parts sent to different towns, and there exhibited as an example of what would-be regicides might expect. 'And so learn traitors that would be.'

Another crime in Henry's reign took place at Coventry's St Mary's Priory when, we are told, 'Hugh, son of Gilbert de Balissall, fell into the Pool of the monks [St Osburg's Pool] of Coventry, and was drowned.' This description seems straightforward but Hugh was also impaled upon a spike of wood as he lay in the water, so this was a suspicious death. The finder of the body was first interviewed and cleared, suspicion subsequently fell upon a cleric named Peter Burum, who pleaded his background saying he should not answer for the charges. The Proctor of the Bishop of Chester appears to have asked for Burum to be handed over to him, and the justices concluded that, 'the twelve jurors and the four neighbouring towns say that the aforesaid Peter threw the aforesaid Hugh into the Pool, so that he fell upon a sharp stake, whereof he died on the third day afterwards. Therefore for such he is delivered to the Proctor.' Burum used his clerical background to good effect as it entitled him to be dealt with by the church, and that usually meant criminals escaped execution.

There were numerous other murders in the reign of Henry although not all in the priory. The Rolls of Justice in Eyre tell us that in 1222, Richard of Keresley was a member of the household of Robert le Scot who had a manor house in the Whitmore/Keresley area called Scot's Hill, possibly on the site of the present Whitmore Park Junior School. Richard stabbed and killed Robert Underwood with a knife and fled. His wife, the unusually named Hawisa testified against him and he was found guilty of murder and outlawed.

In 1232 Matthew Seliman killed Ivo de Tanur with a knife and was outlawed, as was Roger le Seynturer in 1262 who struck Roger Stirthup on the head with a lump of firewood in the house of one Emma. Some ran, as did Richard Labanc who killed William de Essenby in the same year, however he was later taken and hanged at Northampton. Others such as John de Corle acted differently: he struck William le Parber on the head with an axe. Parber died within a fortnight and Corle took up residence in the priory church of St Mary and there claimed sanctuary and admitted his crime to the coroner. Under these circumstances he was protected by the church for forty days, and within that time had to dress in sackcloth, carry a wooden cross and head for the nearest port and from there abjure the realm. If he stayed beyond forty days the law could take him. However, those who did attempt to leave did not always make it out of the country because relatives of their victims sometimes took justice into their own hands, and occasionally headless abjurers would be found in fields only a short distance from their sanctuary.

In the Crown Pleas of 1285 Henry le Moun is mentioned for killing his wife Alice by thrusting a sword through her chest. History does not record his motive, but he ran and was

A set of old Coventry stocks photographed in the Market Square in the 1860s. They can now be seen in the museum.

outlawed. Also, around the same time, William Dunte the miller struck and killed one Nicholas de Wroxhalle, he too was outlawed after he fled. Reginald Abbot of Sowe struck and killed William Gopil with a stick and was also outlawed.

Sometimes those who administered justice were themselves outlawed, as was Ranulf de Kaus, Bailiff of the city of Coventry in 1262. Kaus and another bailiff, Walter le Blunt, accused one Hugh Russell of possessing a stolen horse. They took him and placed him in the stocks for eight days so that as the Eyres state, 'his feet rotted through that imprisonment and later fell from his legs, from which he afterwards died'. Although Hugh le Blunt denied any knowledge of the incident the jury thought otherwise, and believed that le Blunt himself had ordered Kaus to place Russell in the stocks leaving him there long enough for the extreme cold and damp to give him frostbite, causing the loss of his feet and his eventual death. For their deed Kaus was outlawed and le Blunt wearing a habit and claiming to be a cleric, received a short committal to gaol.

CHAPTER 2

Murder by Witchcraft

In the year 1325 a minor favourite of King Edward II died a raving lunatic in Coventry, his name Robert or Richard de Sowe. Sowe's death would be unremarkable had not a certain Robert Mareschal confessed that he had been murdered by witchcraft.

The case resulting from this incident is the earliest witchcraft trial in England of which details are known: the records from it still survive in The National Archives. The events leading up to this trial, began on a snowy December evening in 1324 at the home of John de Nottingham in the Shortley area of Coventry, near the Charterhouse. A group of 'gentlemen' of both Coventry and Warwickshire had gathered there to procure the services of Nottingham, a known necromancer or witch.

Before business was spoken of Nottingham and his assistant Robert Mareschal were sworn to secrecy. They were then told by the spokesman one Robert Latoner that the men gathered here had enemies who overtaxed them in many ways, they included the Prior of Coventry, the Earl of Winchester, Hugh le Despenser and his son and none other than the King himself.

Latoner offered Nottingham £20 for himself and maintenance in any religious house in England and £15 for his assistant if he would kill the king and others using his black arts; Nottingham agreed. It is said that seven days after the Feast of St Nicholas part payment was made and four pounds of wax and two rolls of canvas were supplied to Nottingham to create images.

John de Nottingham, the necromancer, would have looked something like this Victorian engraving.

From this material Nottingham and Mareschal created waxen images of Edward II crowned, the Earl of Winchester, the prior, his Cellarer, Nicholas Crump his Seneschal, Monsieur Hugh and one of Robert de Sowe. At midnight on the Feast of the Holy Cross, Nottingham began to prove his power by taking the image of Sowe and saying an incantation as Mareschal pushed a leaden spike into the image's head. The next morning he sent Mareschal to Sowe's home, probably in Walsgrave-on-Sowe to check on the effects of the previous night's work. Mareschal spoke to various people and discovered that suddenly overnight Robert de Sowe had gone mad, shouting and screaming and unable to recognize those about him.

Mareschal later informed the court that this situation continued until the Sunday before the Feast of the Ascension, when with the agreement of the 'gentlemen' Nottingham had taken the pin from the image's head and pushed it into the heart. Over a week later Sowe stopped his ranting and died. John de Nottingham had proved his power.

The 'gentleman' were informed of the work and it was decided that the hated king himself was soon to become the next victim. However, before this happened Mareschal panicked and turned informer to try to save his own neck. The Sheriff of Warwickshire had Nottingham arrested by personal command of King Edward, and the 'gentlemen', on hearing the news, gave themselves up to the Justice. Mareschal was brought to accuse them but the 'gentlemen' denied any knowledge of the event, pleaded not guilty, and were taken with Nottingham and Mareschal into the custody of Robert de Dumbleton, marshall.

Within a short time a large group of knights and gentlemen from Warwickshire and London paid the bail on Richard Latoner and the gentlemen who then were allowed out of custody on the promise of returning after Easter.

On the fifteenth day after Easter 1325 it was ordered by the Justice that Dumbleton bring John de Nottingham before the king. This was not, however, possible for it was reported that Nottingham had died suddenly while in his custody. Mareschal and the 'gentlemen' were brought forward and the 'gentlemen' cleared of any of the alleged witchcraft or felonies and all rode off into the sunset. Mareschal, however, was returned to prison to await the advice of the court. No record of this 'advice' survives, but it seems unlikely that Mareschal ever saw the light of day again. As for Nottingham, the necromancer would have been considered too dangerous to be allowed to live, which is probably why he so conveniently 'died' in prison – most likely not struck down by illness but by something a bit more solid. So his mouth would have been closed forever, permanently preventing him from testifying against his gentlemen of Coventry and Warwickshire.

Part of the existing west entrance of Coventry Priory, which stood not far from the Sextern, scene of the axe murder.

Murder also took place within the precinct of St Mary's Priory, for apart from the monks' attempted assassination of Bishop Nonant in the twelfth century, the fourteenth century saw the priory as the bloody scene of a triple axe murder in 1394. The rolls of John Houland, coroner of Coventry, reads:

> *It happened at Coventry, on Monday next before the Feast of Epiphany in the seventeenth year of King Richard II, that one John Cristleton, and William, son of the same, John, and Ralph Giffard, servant of the same John, were found dead. An inquest was taken thereon, before the aforesaid coroner, upon view of the bodies of the aforesaid John, William and Ralph, by oaths of ... [twelve jurors] ..., who say upon their oaths, that one Geoffrey Wytles, on Wednesday next before the Feast of Our Lord's Circumcision, in the seventeenth year, aforesaid at Coventry, in the night-time, feloniously entered within the Priory of Coventry in a certain house called Sextern, where the aforesaid John, William and Ralph, dwelled, and did atrociously strike them upon their heads with an axe value 2d., and feloniously did slay and traitorously murder them, and did rob the same John of a sum of money, viz., forty marks, and diverse jewels of the value of £10, which he carried away with him. They also say that the same Geoffrey withdrew immediately after the commission of the felony, and did not carry away with him the said axe.*

The tuppenny axe could be sold on and the money placed into the king's coffers, as the monarch had the right to take cash for all weapons used in assaults and murders. No record appears as to the outcome of this case and we can only assume that this brutal man, Geoffrey Wytles, was declared outlawed and most probably continued to murder and rob in various other parts of the realm.

CHAPTER 3

The Broadgate Murder and other Fifteenth-Century Deeds

On Midsummer night and St Peter's Eve in 1420 Coventry erupted into riots, leaving many injured. To try to control the violence the City Leet issued orders that any man drawing a sword, knife or other weapon would face being fined half a mark for every offence. Butchers and craftsmen were also included, banned from carrying axes, staves or bills or face a twenty-shilling fine and imprisonment. Innkeepers were told that any guest should leave their weapon at the inn before going into the streets. Knights and squires were of course the exception to the rule.

In fifteenth-century Coventry, knights were not uncommon on the streets so the possibility of some armed conflict was always possible. One such incident took place in 1440 when Sir Humphrey Stafford and his son, Richard were in the city visiting Lady Shrewsbury, wife of the great Lancastrian soldier hero John Talbot. Stafford held the title of Duke of Buckingham from 1444, and was one of the richest men in England, a descendant of a great grandson of King Edward III. Despite his titles and riches he also had enemies, some of whom waited for him as night fell in Broadgate. As he returned from Lady Shrewsbury's

The Duke of Gloucester and Earl of Warwick, two knights known to Coventry and Buckingham and Harcourt.

lodgings he and his son, Richard, a knight who had fought in France, were confronted by Sir Robert Harcourt and his men. Words were exchanged and a fight broke out.

After the event John Northwood wrote to Viscount Beaumont of the incident saying:

> *Sir Robert smote him* [Sir Humphrey] *a great stroke on the head with his sword, and Richard with his dagger hastily went toward him, and as he stumbled one of Harcourt's men smote him in the back with a knife … His father rode towards him and his men run before him and in going down off his horse … not knowing who was behind him he was smote on the head with an edged weapon of unknown type. With that he fell down and his son fell down before him as good as dead.*

The fight ended with the vicious wounding of Sir Humphrey and the death of Richard and the death of two of Harcourt's men. The fight is believed to have been an old quarrel between the families. As nobles were involved nothing came of the death; Harcourt, the instigator of the attack, walked away from the murder. Family honour was not settled for another twenty years when Harcourt was ambushed and murdered by a Stafford.

Other notable nobles died in Coventry around this time, for example Earl Rivers, Richard Woodville, and his son John Woodville, in 1469. The Woodvilles came from a minor Northamptonshire family and rose quickly to power when Richard's daughter, Elizabeth, secretly married King Edward IV. Through his new royal connection in 1448 he was created Lord Rivers, then a knight of the garter, royal councillor and seneschal of Aquitaine and lieutenant of Calais. He was subsequently made an earl, lord treasurer and constable of England

An ancient engraving showing Richard Woodville, Earl Rivers, presenting a book to King Edward IV.

much to the annoyance of other lords. John Woodville became Duke of Norfolk and the rest of the Woodville clan grabbed what they could, becoming one of the most disliked families in the realm. Richard and John were later taken by rioters at Chepstow and given into the hands of Richard Neville, the Earl of Warwick, who was secretly starting riots and rebellions and scheming Edward's downfall after failing to control him. Warwick had the two members of the Yorkist royal family brought to Coventry and beheaded on Gosford Green.

The following year the City *Annals* informs us that others followed that same fate. One Chapman was beheaded and his head stuck on a pole and placed above Bablake Gate, why, and who he was we are not informed. The same source tells us that in 1472 there was a rising in Kent and London Bridge was set on fire and, 'The King went and took the Captains, and beheaded them in Coventry.' This was no doubt a Lancastrian rebellion against Yorkist Edward IV and most likely the leaders of this rebellion were executed in Coventry because of the city's close Lancastrian connections as the seat of the royal court of the Lancastrian King Henry VI for nearly three years.

In 1487 King Henry VII was on the throne but many others made claims on it. One is recorded in the City *Annals* as ending his days in Coventry, the *Annals* say:

> *The king came to Coventry to see the playes on St. Peter's daye. Hee lodged at Sir Robert Onlyes in Smithford Street. On Wensday after St. Peter's day Tho. Harrington was beheaded on ye Conduite by the Bull and buryed att the Grayfryers. He called himself the Duke of Clarence's son.*

Harrington was captured after the battle of Stoke, probably a noted Yorkist. The gentleman who claimed to be the son of the Duke of Clarence was in fact Lambert Simnel and not Harrington as the *Annals* claim. This confusion may have arisen because of various rewritings of the *Annals*.

The use of Coventry as an execution ground continued in 1495 when Sir Henry Mumford and Sir Robert Mallory, after receiving judgement in London, were sent to Coventry. Here under the Binley Gallows on the junction of Brandon Road and Brinklow Road the two lords were beheaded before a

A fifteenth-century execution taking place. The site of Harrington's execution is now a branch of Marks & Spencer.

large crowd. Afterwards Mumford's head was displayed on Bablake Gate and Mallory's on Bishop Gate. The friars of Greyfriars took the bodies and buried them and later also acquired the heads. Interestingly when the present Central Methodist Hall was being built in 1931 John Bailey Shelton excavated part of the site of the church, unearthing the north transept and part of the burial ground. Here he found two bodiless skulls encased in clay, no doubt those of these once illustrious lords.

Two less notable characters John Heires and William Lingham were executed for robbing St Mary's Guildhall. A third person involved in the event, but not mentioned in the *Annals*, was Thomas Walton originally described as a yeoman. The guild's records state that these men were

> *tried before John Lusterly, Mayor of Coventry, and other justices, on the charge that he* [Walton], *with other persons unknown, did on April 24, 1445, break into St. Mary's Hall by night and stole therefrom a standing gilt silver cup, two silver bowls with two silver gilt covers, two silver spice dishes, small silver gilt table spoon, two knoppes* [spoons with decorative finials], *a silver trumpet, a silver bowl cup and cover, two silver cups, four gilt silver spoons, a silver standing cup, a silver goblet, a silver salt cellar with cover, and twenty-four silver spoons, the property of the Trinity Guild. Walton was also indicted for stealing 13s. 1d. in money on October 27, following. Having been found guilty by the jury, he was sentenced to be hanged, upon which he claimed benefit of the clergy, saying he was of the clergy* [and therefore could not be hanged]. *In consequence of this claim he was delivered over to the Ordinaries of the Diocese, and the Bishop issued his writ to the Archdeacon and the priests of the two parish churches in Coventry, dated October 11, 1447, directing them on each Sunday and the festival at the time of mass, in the churches, in the market of the city, and other frequented places, to make public proclamation, that if anyone was able to accuse Walton of these charges, or to object to his purgation, he should appear before the Bishop or his vicar general in Eccleshall Church, on Tuesday, November 28 following, and there bring forward his objections.*

Walton's plea was successful and he walked away from the crime. His accomplices, Heires and Lingham, however felt the full weight of the law, culminating with them being hanged before thousands late in 1447.

CHAPTER 4

The Coventry Martyrs

In the early years of the reign of Henry VIII England was in religious turmoil. In Coventry the seeds of this turmoil were sown many years earlier in the 1380s when local man John Wycliffe tried to break the hold of the established Catholic Church by printing the Bible in English. Lollardism, the fruit of his work, was quickly established in the city and Coventry was described as a 'nest of heresy'.

Lollards began to be persecuted under Henry and in 1510, the year of his only visit to the city, ten Lollards accused of heresy were made to carry faggots of wood before the people in Cross Cheaping. All recanted except Joan Ward who was burnt at the stake in the Little Park in a sandstone pit called the Park Hollows.

In 1519 another group of innocent locals were persecuted by the Church for daring to say the Lord's Prayer, the Ten Commandments and the Creed in English. For this heresy the

The remains of the Greyfriars Church and Friary (right) where the children of Coventry martyrs were taken for examination.

Bishop of Coventry, one Geoffrey Blyth, ordered that Alice Lansdail, a widow also called Smith (her maiden name), Thomas Lansdail, her brother-in-law, a hosier, Hosea Hawkins, a skinner, Thomas Wrexham or Wrigsham, a glover; Robert Hockett, Thomas Bond, both shoemakers and Robert Silksby should be 'purified' by the Church, in other words publically burned at the stake in the Little Park with the Church's blessing. Their children were taken from them and placed under the care of the Greyfriars at whose friary (at the bottom of Greyfriars Lane) they underwent examination by the Warden and were told that if they wished to avoid the fate of their parents they were never to meddle with the Lord's Prayer, Creed and Ten Commandments.

Through lack of evidence Alice Lansdail was discharged and when Simon Norton the Bishop's Sumner was seeing her home he felt a parchment hidden in her sleeve bearing the Lord's Prayer and the Ten Commandments in English. This she was either given as soon as she left prison or alternatively it was planted upon her. She was immediately re-arrested, taken back and later condemned to join the others. Robert Silksby managed to escape but two years later was taken and ended his days in the flaming pit at the Park Hollows, for denying the Real Presence. All the property and goods of these unfortunates were taken by the Sheriff, leaving their families destitute.

Later, after Henry's split from Rome, the tables would reverse and the English Bible became predominant. This changed again during the reign of his daughter Mary. Shortly after she was crowned in 1553 she ordered the mayor of Coventry to apprehend the Reverend Hugh Symonds, vicar of St Michael's, who had commented during a sermon on the Queen's religious ideals.

Coventry magistrates were ordered to put down the Protestant faith in the city, this did not, however, totally succeed for few were real Catholics and many continued, until more enlightened times, to hold sermons in the fields.

Soon Mary began her persecution in which innocent godly men would die, and she quickly acquired the title, 'Bloody Mary' by which she became known to history. Coventry witnessed this first hand with the burning of Lawrence Saunders in 1555. Saunders was born in 1519 at Harrington in Northamptonshire and was educated at Eton and King's College, Cambridge. He was subsequently apprenticed to a London merchant, but finding the life unsuitable, returned to King's to continue his studies, especially of the scriptures. In 1547 Saunders was ordained and in 1553 became the Rector of All Hallows in Bread Street, London.

After the accession of Mary, Saunders preached against 'popish doctrine', and later preached against the newly established Church calling it a 'papist serpent'. On that same afternoon on returning to his church he was arrested and thrown into prison for fifteen months awaiting the pleasure of an interview with the Bishop of London.

The day came and Saunders, charged with treason and heresy, was brought before the bishop, who said to him, 'Notwithstanding the Queen's proclamation to the contrary, you have continued to preach.' Saunders replied that these were perilous times and he had exhorted his flock to stand steadfast in the doctrine they had learned, meaning the Protestant faith.

Saunders added that he preached what his conscience told him, to which the bishop replied, 'This your conscience could make our Queen a bastard, or misbegotten; would it not I pray you?' To which Saunders replied, 'We do not declare or say that the queen is base or misbegotten, neither go about any such matter. But let those take care whose writings are yet in the hands of men witnessing the same.' This was an illusion to the bishop's own book which he wrote in the reign of Henry claiming the princess was illegitimate.

Saunders, final remark was that he only taught the purity of the Word and said he would pray for the bishop's conversion. The interview came to an abrupt halt and Saunders was dragged back to prison. There he remained for one year and three months before he was once again brought before the clergy. This time he was offered mercy if he would give up his 'abominable heresies and false doctrine'. Saunders refused their demands repeating what he had said previously. At the end of the interview Bishop Bonner produced a document attacking the Catholic Church and falsely accused Saunders of writing it and calling him a heretic. He then returned him to prison, had him excommunicated, and the Bishop of London came to 'degrade him'. When this was done Saunders is reported as saying, 'I thank God I am not of your Church.'

On the following day he was delivered to the Queen's Guard who brought him to Coventry to be burnt. Coventry was no doubt chosen because of its great connection with Lollardism, and apparently Saunders was well known in the city and may have lived here. He was placed amongst the other prisoners in the common gaol and there spent the night in prayer. On the following morning (8 February 1555) Foxe wrote in his *Book of Martyrs*:

> *he was led to the place of execution in the park, without the city. He went in an old gown and shirt, and barefooted and he often fell flat on the ground and prayed. When he was come nigh to the place, the officer who was appointed to see the execution done, said that he was one of those who marred the queen's realm with false doctrine and heresy, 'Wherefore though hast deserved death,' said he; 'but yet, if thou revoke thine heresies, the queen hath pardoned thee; if not, yonder fire is prepared for thee.'*

To this Saunders answered:

> *It is not I, nor my fellow preachers of God's truth, that have hurt the queen's realm, but it is yourself, and such as you are, who have always resisted God's holy word, it is you who hath and do mar the queen's realm. I do hold no heresies but the doctrine of God, the blessed Gospel of Christ; that I hold, that I believe, that I have taught, and that I will never revoke.*

With that his tormenter cried, 'Away with him.'

Saunders continued on his last walk and again fell to the ground and prayed and when he reached the stake he held it, kissed it, saying, 'Welcome the cross of Christ, welcome everlasting life.' Then he was chained to the stake and more faggots of wood were added. The fire grew and began the slow and horrifically painful burning of Saunders' body before

The burning of Lawrence Saunders from Foxe's Book of Martyrs, *1555.*

death released him, or as Foxe put it, 'the fire being put to him, full sweetly he slept in the Lord'.

Another account gives more graphic information stating that, 'Being then fastened, and fire applied to the stake, he was burnt to ashes; but the wood being green, he, for a considerable time endured much pain.'

The next innocent to suffer was Robert Glover, educated at Eton and Oxford. In the beginning of 1555 according to Foxe the Bishop of Coventry ordered the Mayor and Officers of Coventry to arrest John Glover of Mancetter Hall on suspicion of heresy. The mayor who disagreed with the persecution sent a private warning to John Glover before the Sheriff sent his men. John escaped with his brother William just before their arrival.

Foxe picks up the story, 'But when John could not be found, one of the officers going in the upper chamber found Robert, the other brother lying on his bed, and sick of a severe disease; who was immediately brought before the Sheriff.' Realizing he was not the man they wanted the Sheriff, Richard Hopkins, was initially going to release him but was persuaded to hold on and await the Bishop's coming. Later Hopkins was ordered to put Glover to the torture but he refused point blank, a refusal, which would later lead him to prison.

Eleven days later Glover was brought out of prison to face charges, despite the fact that as he himself stated, it was contrary to the laws of the realm, 'They having neither statute law, proclamation, letter, warrant, nor commandment for my apprehension.' They tried to lay the matter on the Summoner, but he would have none of it for the warrant was for John not Robert.

Foxe recorded Robert Glover's own words:

The second day after the bishop's coming to Coventry, Master Warren came to the Guildhall, and commanded the Chief Gaoler to carry me to the bishop. I laid to Master Warren's charge the cruel seeking of my death; and when he would have excused himself, I told him he could not wipe his hands so; as he was guilty of my blood before God as though he had murdered me with his own hands ... And so he departed from me saying, I need not fear if I would be of his belief ... When I came before the bishop in one Denton's house he began by protesting that he was my bishop, and willed me to submit myself. I said to him, 'I have not come to accuse myself; what have you to lay to my charge?'

The bishop asked Glover if he was learned to which he replied, 'smally learned', and the chancellor informed the bishop that he was a master of arts. The bishop then laid a charge against Glover that he failed to attend church. Glover being new to the area knew this was a fact the bishop could not prove and angered at the trumped up charge said he would not attend 'their church' as long as 'their mass' was used. He then asked the bishop to show him one 'jot' in the Scripture for the defence of the mass.

The interrogation continued and the chancellor accused Glover of being arrogant and sent him back to the gaol. The bishop then decided to return to Lichfield and ordered Glover's removal there, of this Robert wrote to his wife:

Certain sergeants and constables of Coventry being appointed to convey us [Cornelius Bungay] *to Lichfield, to be delivered there to one Jepcot, the chancellor's man, we were commanded to mount on horseback about eleven or twelve o'clock on Friday, being market day, that we might be the more gazed and wondered at; and to kindle the people's hearts more against us.*

Glover was again interrogated in Lichfield and kept in a small cell, where, 'I was allowed no help, neither night nor day, nor company of any man, notwithstanding my great sickness; nor yet paper, nor ink, nor books, saving my New Testament in Latin, and a prayer book, which I privately procured'. Not wishing to return to the bishop's Church, Robert Glover was declared a heretic and it was ordered that he be returned to Coventry for execution. While in gaol he wrote to his wife Mary saying:

I thank you most heartily, most loving wife, for your letters sent to me in my imprisonment. I read them with tears, I say for joy and gladness, that God had wrought in you so merciful a work. ... Wherefore, I thought it my bounden duty, both to God and man ... to set aside all fear, perils and dangers ... and persuaded all that professed God's word, manfully to persist in the defence of the same, not with sword and violence but with suffering and loss of life rather than to defile themselves again with the whorish abomination of the Roman Antichrist.

Robert Glover spent his last night alive in Coventry Gaol praying in the company of Austen Berner, later Rector of Southam who ministered to him and promised that God would be with him as he went to his death. The following day (19 September 1555) Glover was led to the stake down Little Park Street and as he approached the Hollow he suddenly clapped his hands crying 'Austen, he is come. He is come.' Robert Glover did not die alone for with him in the flames was Cornelius Bungay, a Coventry capper, who is said to have been condemned for 'holding, maintaining, arguing and teaching' heretical doctrine in both Coventry and Lichfield.

Coventry's sympathetic sheriff who had wanted to release Glover was Richard Hopkins of the Palace Yard, who at that

The burning of Robert Glover and Cornelius Bungay in the Little Park.

time was also under investigation for refusing to execute Saunders. While under scrutiny it is believed that Hopkins proved himself a Protestant by giving a copy of the New Testament to a condemned felon and for this and his refusal to follow orders he himself was arrested and committed to his own gaol. He spent some time in the Fleet Prison in London before leaving England with his wife and children to go into exile in Switzerland. On Mary's death he returned to Coventry.

Despite the death of Robert Glover without warrant the Bishop of Coventry and Lichfield ordered a new search for John Glover. He again escaped and this time his wife Agnes was imprisoned in his stead. John hid in the woods near his home and soon contacted an 'ague' from which he died. Later his body was found and buried in the churchyard, but the chancellor hearing of this ordered that it be exhumed and thrown over the wall into the public highway, there to be left to rot. The chancellor was informed by a local spokesman that the body had been in the ground for six weeks and 'smelled, none would abide the stench'. It was then ordered that Glover be pronounced a damned soul and twelve month later his bones were unearthed and thrown into the common highway so 'that carts and horse may tread upon them'.

The same problem occurred with the last brother, William. When he died the curate of the church not wishing to bury him wrote to the 'good' bishop who replied:

> *Understanding that one Glover, a heretic is dead ... a rebel against our holy faith and religion ... and never required to be reconciled to our mother holy church ... I thought it good ... to command the curate ... that he should not be buried with a Christian man's burial ... nor speak to have him buried in holy ground ... but I do charge and command that he is not buried either in the church, or within the limits of the churchyard ... I do charge those that brought the body to the place, to carry it away again ... or they will answer at their peril.*
> *At Ecclesch, this 6th September, A.D. 1555.*
> *By your ordinary*
> *RADULPH, COVENTRY AND LICHFIELD.*

By that time William Glover's body had begun to decompose and, 'they were forced to draw it with horses into the broom-field, and there he was buried'.

Two other Coventry men were burned for their faith, although not in Coventry. The first, John Carelesse a weaver, was arrested in Coventry in November 1554 for lewd and seditious behaviour. He was later described by his inquisitor as, 'one of the pleasantest Protestants I have ever met'. He spent two years in Coventry Gaol with his wife and child staying with him. He was well liked by the gaolers and allowed to leave the gaol regularly and to practice and take part in the

Coventry Mystery Plays. He was then sent to London and there found guilty of heresy. While there he wrote a letter to his friends, 'My friends in Coventry have put the Council in remembrance of me, not six days ago, saying, I am more worthy to be burned than any that was burned yet. God's blessing in their hearts for this good report.' The worthy John Carelesse did not however face the fire but died during his

The Martyr's Memorial erected in 1910 two hundred yards from the site of the burnings. The memorial was later moved a short distance to accommodate the ring road.

confinement, probably of prison fever. It is said by some sources that his body was then buried in a dunghill!

Another Coventry man who did burn in London was Jocelyn Palmer, son of a Coventry mayor and Fellow of Magdalen College, Oxford. Palmer spoke Latin and Greek and unlike his fellow sufferers was an ex-Catholic who, seeing the bravery of Ridley and Latimer at the stake, changed his faith. After acquiring his new faith he was thrown out of Oxford, obtained a post as a schoolmaster, but was then cast from that post as well. He was later arrested and for his new beliefs burned at the stake in July 1557.

At the bottom of Little Park Street stands a monumental cross, erected in remembrance of the Coventry martyrs who died horrifically because of their beliefs. In 1854 the keeper of Quinton Park, William Mansfield, made a discovery in the old Park Hollows in the Martyrs Field, he later wrote:

I was digging in the Park Hollows; and when I had dug down about six feet from the surface I came to some very black soil, altogether different from that which I dug through. I also found some charred or burnt wood, some cinders, and pieces of bright coal. I also found a number of bones, and a piece of silk, which might have been part of a dress, close by the bones. I had got down to the rock in which was what appeared to be a grave, and the bones and piece of silk were in this grave.

CHAPTER 5

Mayors and Murder

O ne of the first major crimes in Coventry recorded in the sixteenth century was committed in 1523 when Pratt and Slouth were arrested in Coventry for treason. Under torture the men also confessed their ambitious intent to murder the mayor, Julius Nethermill and his brethren; to have robbed and taken St Mary's Hall and to have taken Kenilworth Castle. History does not record exactly who these men were and why they wanted to take the buildings, was this some form of conspiracy or were they tortured into confessing anything, fact or fantasy.

Significantly the men were taken to London for judgement, then sent back to Coventry for execution. The City *Annals* describe it thus:

> *they were drawn on a slead to the Gallows and were hanged, drawn and quartered, the head of Slouth was set on New Gate with a leg and a shoulder and the Rest of him was bestowed on Bishop Gate and the Head of Pratt was set on Bablake Gate with a leg and shoulder and the rest of him was bestowed on Grayfriar Gate.*

The ambitious Pratt and Slouth wanted to take Kenilworth Castle.

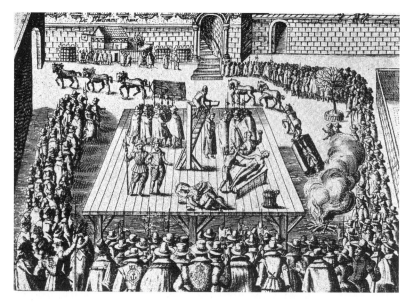

Men being hung, drawn and quartered in the sixteenth century.

Three years later the *Annals* records another ambitious pair, Pickering Clarke of the King's Larder and Anthony Manville, a gentleman. They, with other conspirators meant to rob the king's tax collectors, raise an army to take Kenilworth Castle and make battle against the king. For this they were hung, drawn and quartered in London while their fellow conspirators were sent to Coventry for execution. The date in the *Annals* may be wrong for this event is most likely to have taken place in 1525 when Henry VIII needed money for his war chest which was empty and a tax was instigated by Wolsey called the 'amicable grant'. None found it very amicable as some who collected it used threats, soon parts of the country were up in arms and this is where Clarke and Manville come in, trying to mirror a rebellion in Suffolk by taking the tax money back from the collectors and attempting to start a rebellion in Warwickshire.

In that same year of 1525 the commons of Coventry rose up and pulled down fences and hedges probably at Whitley, which had enclosed the old common land. When the mob returned to the city they locked New Gate against the city chamberlains.

During which it is said the mayor was nearly, 'smothered in the throng'. Despite his near-death experience the mayor supported the commoners and quickly found himself arrested and thrown from his high office, subsequently being sent down to London to be questioned by Cardinal Wolsey with others, forty of whom were imprisoned. This incident had its effect on the corporation for at the next city leet meeting it was ordered that common land recently enclosed should be opened up again.

Coventry's Tudor mayors appear to have been prone to getting themselves into trouble, but none can match up to the stain put on the mayoralty of one John Harford. One day in 1569 Harford was walking his two greyhounds in the fields when he came upon William Heeley, an embroiderer walking with his wife and mother and their little pet spaniel. Harford's greyhounds ran at the dog and began worrying it and Heeley in a panic tried to beat them off. Seeing this Harford, Coventry's most respected citizen, ran forward and, with his walking staff, struck Heeley a desperate blow across the back. What happened afterwards is not recorded but after suffering two weeks of pain William Heeley died, and Coventry's mayor became a murderer.

Queen Elizabeth was informed of the event and wrote back to the Recorder and Aldermen, saying:

Trusty and well beloved, we greet you well. We perceive by letter written from you unto our right trusty and well beloved cousin and counsellor, the Earl of Leicester, whereof he hath made report unto us the late mischance happened to the Mayor of that our city of Coventry, being charged with the death of one of our subjects of our said city, for which he is committed to ward. And like as we find it reasonable that his cause be tried and ordered by the ordinary course of justice and the laws of our realm; without any particular regard of persons, or of private respect; so do not we think convenient that our said city should remain without a head or governor till the accustomed time of the election of a new Mayor there … We let you therefore wit our pleasure and commandment is that upon the receipt of these our letters … you shall forthwith proceed as well to the deprivation of the said

Mayor from his mayoralty, as also the election of another in his stead … we mean not to prejudice the cause of the said late Mayor, or that any hold or advantage should be thereby taken to enforce any matter against him … if by order of law the fact of your Mayor shall deserve death, our meaning is, that before any execution thereof done, you should certify us of your proceedings in the trial.

Given under our signet, at our town of Southampton, the 8th day of September, the 11th year of our reign. Elizabeth Regina.

Harford was put on trial and found guilty of the death of William Heeley but gained a pardon by authority of Heeley's wife after paying her a substantial, but unspecified sum.

Queen Elizabeth ordered the removal of Harford from office.

CHAPTER 6

Murder in Cromwell's Coventry

I n 1641, a year before the Civil War began, Coventry discovered the existence of its first and only known serial killer. A man simply described as 'Johnson', was an inmate in Bond's Hospital in Hill Street, and got on with few of his fellow inmates. Those who displeased Johnson all died from poison administered by him. Whether Johnson poisoned all twelve at the same time or one by one is not recorded, but whatever happened his foul deed finally caught up with him and Johnson the Poisoner poisoned himself. His body was originally buried in the churchyard of Holy Trinity, but because of objections, he was exhumed and his body taken and buried as a traditional suicide, pinned down in the roadside outside Cook Street Gate.

Bond's Hospital (left) home to a serial poisoner attached to Bablake School.

Law and order generally appear to have prevailed in Cromwellian Coventry as few crimes are recorded. One in 1649, the year of King Charles's execution, is recorded in the City *Annals*, it reads:

> *On Christmas Eve the butchers rose, and Howes, one of the principal of the Companie killed a souldier that came to gather excise, for which many of them were imprisoned, and Howes tried for his life, but was found guilty of manslaughter. He lived above 40 years after and died an old man in Babelake Hospitall but never prospered after ye aforesaid fact.*

The butchers who concentrated around both Great Butcher Row and Little Butcher Row were noted as standing up against authority. When the puritans tried to demolish the Coventry Cross the butchers gathered, armed themselves, and drove them away.

Another murder happened on Friday, 18 October 1695 and was again reported in the City *Annals*. It appears that between

William Bennett was murdered here where Broadgate enters Cross Cheaping.

twelve and one in the morning Nicholas Lambe, an excise man accompanied by William Whittaker and Samuel Wickes and two corporals of Captain Porter's troop, left the *Star Inn* after having a drink and walked down Much Park Street, Dead Lane, Little Park Street, High Street smashing windows. They entered Broadgate and on approaching Coventry Cross the five men attacked another man beating him in the street. The noise drew the attention of William Bennet, a dyer and City Constable and other men of the City Watch who were in the nearby Mayor's Parlour. Bennet called the men to stop demanding they be civil and was immediately killed by a sword thrust that went through his armpit and came out of his neck. The men were pursued and taken and Lambe, Whittaker and Wickes were put on trial on 30 March 1696. The three men were found guilty of murder and sentenced to death. Wickes and Lambe were hanged, probably on Whitley Common, on 8 April while Whittaker was reprieved and pardoned. The fate of the two soldiers is not mentioned as justice for them was kept strictly within the military and not a matter of public record.

On Sunday, 20 October 1695 William Bennet was buried in St Michael's churchyard amid a numerous company, including the mayor and aldermen of the city.

CHAPTER 7

Soldiers Shot in the Park

Throughout the eighteenth century, before the Barracks was built, Coventry was a city in which army regiments were billeted. Soldiers were billeted around various inns in the city and officers often stayed at more well-to-do houses. The presence of the military in the city led to occasional incidents but few appear to be recorded.

Not all members of the forces chose to be there for on 1 March 1756 the Privy Council issued a circular asking the Mayor, Alderman John Hewitt, in His Majesty's name to 'search for and seize all seamen and seafaring men fit to serve in the navy'. This was a lucrative business for the men seizing them could earn twenty shillings for each man and sixpence per mile to take them from Coventry to Leicester.

Over the days that followed seven were impressed by force and four volunteered. These men, however, not being willing to be forced back to sea, had to be taken to Leicester by men of Colonel Lambton's Regiment which was stationed in the city. They would remain under guard until they were safely at sea.

Things had not changed, except possibly for the public's perception, by 1779 as the *Coventry Mercury* of 17 May reported:

On Friday last, was exhibited in the streets of this city, a scene, which no doubt must have given very painful sensations to every stickler for English liberty. A number of impressed men to the amount of twenty, chained two and two, with one continuous chain, passing from the first to the last, was driven along by their humane *keepers, like a gang of galley slaves. Sure it was the unusualness of the sight which raised indignant horror in the breast of every spectator, perhaps when the scene has been acted over more frequently, we shall with less disgust or total apathy behold a brother and a friend, torn from all that is dear and delightful to him and hurried away in irons.*

While stationed in the city soldiers occasionally deserted, this offence was not taken at all lightly and could mean a death sentence. The year 1757 appears to have been particularly busy in this respect. The *Coventry Mercury* carried many advertisements calling upon citizens to apprehend deserters for a reward of twenty shillings each. One, twenty-four-year-old Thomas Meeks, was described as five feet four, born in Staffordshire, but enlisted in Coventry. He was by trade a locksmith, had very dark brown eyes and hair and what is described as a, 'remarkable cut under each eye'.

On 21 March the *Mercury* reported, 'This day a special court martial is to be held upon two deserters, one of which (as he has deserted several times) it's thought will be shot.' And a soldier makes the news again on 28 March for it was reported that:

> *At a public house in this city on Saturday night last, a fray happened between a soldier and two other men, in which the soldier cut one of them with a hanger* [a short curved sword] *in the face, in so desperate a manner that his life is despaired of. The watchmen coming in, the soldier struck at 'em, and accidentally cut off one of his fingers. He has been since taken into custody.*

As this event was not mentioned again the gentleman in fear of his life must have recovered, or the event may have been kept out of the public eye, as so often happened when such incidents involved the army.

On 4 April the *Mercury* stated that: 'We hear that on Tuesday se'nnight a soldier is to be shot in the Park for desertion.' The actual execution was reported on the 18 April thus:

> *On Saturday last about noon, a soldier belonging to General Steuart's Regiment, quartered in this city, was shot for desertion in the Park. He had been condemned to be shot for desertion once before, and was reprieved. – He behaved very penitent and acknowledged he deserved to die.*

The execution took place in the Park against a surviving section of the old city wall outside Little Park Gate at the end of Little

Little Park Gate, the last thing the soldiers saw before their execution against the city wall. Coventry City Libraries, Local Studies

Park Street. This was not the first or last, so it seems likely that that particular section of wall was pock-marked by musket shot.

On 27 June the *Mercury* reported a lesser punishment for desertion: 'On Wednesday morning last a soldier belonging to General Steuart's Regiment, received a thousand lashes, and was afterwards drummed out of the regiment with a halter about his neck, for desertion.' The following day another soldier received the same punishment. Such a punishment must have lasted for hours and in itself could prove fatal.

The army were not getting soft for the same report went on to say:

On Saturday last, George Robinson (of the said regiment) was shot in the Park for desertion, he being an old offender. He died very penitent and in a manner very much becoming a person in his unhappy circumstances. He desired the soldiers to take warning by his untimely end, and to avoid keeping company with lewd women, to whom he chiefly attributed his death, saying that he had often sold his linen, &c, to supply them with money, and then being afraid to face his officers, was the occasion of his deserting.

It continued, 'It is thought that another soldier who is now in custody, and was to have been shot about eight months ago, but reprieved, and has since deserted, will be shot when the regiment gets into camp.'

Some deserters did not give in so easily as the *Coventry Mercury* of 7 June 1762 testified:

On Wedsday night last, seven deserters who were confined in the dungeon belonging to the gaol of this city, found means notwithstanding they had irons on, and a guard placed continually at the gaol door, to make their escape by undermining part of the wall and making their way into and going through a house adjoining, known by the name of the Blackamoor's Head. There was another deserter confined with them, but he did not choose to attempt to escape.

Soldiers did not always protect, they also occasionally murdered and sometimes robbed. In May 1779 four soldiers robbed a farrier as he made his way home down the Kenilworth Road. One was later taken, but was subsequently discharged owing to lack of evidence. This was often the case for few locals wanted to prosecute a soldier simply because they feared repercussions.

A few years earlier in 1772 Adam Tilley, who was visiting relatives in Coventry, spent an evening at the *Unicorn* in the company of one Corporal Jackson and some of his men, spending seven shillings on drinks for them. The men all agreed to share a room for the night, however when Tilley went to bed Jackson refused to let him share the room. On his second demand Corporal Jackson drew his sword and stabbed Tilley in several places. A surgeon was brought but Tilley was feared to be at death's door. Whether he died or not is not recorded but Jackson was committed to gaol but later released.

On one occasion in July 1802 a number of soldiers in Coventry Barracks were accused of attacking men, women and children. A copy of this charge was sent by a Coventry solicitor to the regiment's commander-in-chief, the Prince Regent. It read:

> *Yesterday was the day appointed for chairing Messrs. Barlow and Jeffreys, during the whole of which the soldiers belonging to Captain Barlow's regiment (the King's Own or 1st Dragoon Guards) were extremely riotous and most unmercifully beat and* [paper damaged] *many of the inhabitants without the smallest provocation on their parts.*
>
> *In the evening, without the smallest appearance of riot or disturbance, the troops were let loose from the Barracks, first one by one (mounted and swords drawn) and afterwards in a body, headed by Cornets Addison and Bracebridge, during which the most wanton cruelty ever known was practiced on the peaceful inhabitants. The troops indiscriminately cut and hewed down men, women and children, forced themselves into houses, and brutally beat the persons therein. In fact it is impossible for me to describe the enormities committed. Great numbers are badly wounded and much injury is otherwise sustained. I happened to be out of Coventry, but at my return, about half-past eight, at the risk of my own life, I went to the Barracks and requested the troops to be immediately called in, with which request the officer of the day, Cornet Addison and Mr. Williamson, a magistrate, immediately complied …*

News of the letter reached the mayor via the War Office and he wrote personally to the Prince Regent to inform him of what 'really' happened, stating that:

> *On the morning of the 22nd of July the chairing of Mr. Jeffrey and Capt. Barlow, the returned members for the city, took place. The band of the regiment, at the request of several of the principle*

Coventry Barracks which, around 1880, appears relatively unchanged since its erection in 1793.

inhabitants attended the procession. Several of the privates, about 16 in number (unarmed), assisted in leading the horses of the band, who conducted themselves throughout the day in a most orderly and peaceable manner.

On the procession entering Spon Street a very large mob of persons in the interest of Mr. Bird and Mr. Moore (the unsuccessful candidates) were assembled for the avowed purpose of attacking and insulting the members. The chair of Mr. Jeffrey's was soon surrounded, stones thrown in various directions, threats and imprecations, the most horrid, uttered and at length such acts of riot and violence committed as to induce the magistrates to request a small detachment of the regiment to be in readiness to restore the peace ...

An attempt was made by one of the mob to dismount one of the band, which was resisted by the privates leading the horses and some blows were struck on both sides ... Had not this attack been made on the band, not a soldier would have stirred from his post

... In the afternoon of the same day a great number of partisans of Mr. Bird and Mr. Moore dined together at Radford ... and in the evening it was given out that a grand mock chairing was to take place at this village of a man of the name of Sammons (a parish pauper) who they pretended was returned as the member ... The mock chairing took place and of course brought together a very large number of persons [around 1,000], *the most violent and disorderly of the partisans ... the banditti returned from Radford to Coventry preceded by two drums and two fifes, insulting and beating every person they met wearing the cockade of Mr. Jeffreys and Captain Barlow.*

A soldier near the market place was violently beaten by them, thrown down, and kicked most cruelly. On their approaching the barracks the Rouges March was beat, and several of the privates standing there were attacked ... Many of the inhabitants were also seriously hurt ... a magistrate deemed it necessary to interfere. A small detachment of military was therefore ordered out and the mob instantly dispersed ... The magistrate ... was himself assaulted ... No information has reached my ear of any one person being seriously wounded or even wounded at all.

Whatever the truth of the matter, some citizens did get attacked by the military under the auspices of the military commander of the day and the mayor, who were both, by the way, supporters of the winning candidates Jeffreys and Captain Barlow. Coventry elections at the time were known nationally as being notoriously violent, but this was the first time the violence had involved the military.

CHAPTER 8

The Murder of Thomas Edwards 1765

In the late eighteenth century Alderman John Hewitt Junior, three times Mayor of Coventry, Justice of the Peace and thief taker, published two books containing information concerning some of his most important criminal cases. Regarding the murder of Thomas Edwards he wrote:

The following account of the most horrid and barbarous murder and robbery, committed near this city of Coventry, on Friday the 18th of March 1765. Thomas Edwards, John Spencer and John Green of the parish of Stoneleigh, going home from market late that evening, were attacked by three persons in the fields near Whoberley House, about three hundred yards distance from the high road leading to Allesley ... Thomas Edwards being quite sober made a stout resistance with a stick, received nine desperate wounds on his head and face, his skull being fractured, he died the Monday following.

The other two being in liquor were struck down, without seeing, either the two men ... each received three dangerous wounds on their heads, and after having been robbed of their money ... were left senseless on the ground. Edwards, though so inhumanely treated recovered his senses after some time and was able to get to a house about a quarter of a mile distant ... and soon after became speechless and remained so until his death. The other two wounded men after some time recovered themselves and got home to their families, but being in liquor could give no account of this cruel affair.

The following day a young boy out walking his spaniel at the scene found a cock of a pistol with its flint still in it and a piece of ramrod lying near a large pool of blood, enough it was said, 'as if a pig had been stuck'. News of the event and the pistol fragment came to the parlour of John Hewitt, who later wrote:

I immediately suspected either that some of Lord Pembroke's dragoons or some other discharged men from some other corps were concerned in this affair. The three troops of the above, lately quartered here, having marched that morning … for Warwick, I immediately set out after them, in order to apply to the officers … to get a strict examination made into every man's pistol.

On Hewitt's arrival the inspection was made but no damaged pistol was found. While there he discussed with Major Barber his suspicions about some of his men as a similar robbery had taken place when the troops were based in Kilmarnock. Hewitt pointed out the similarities with attacks in and around Coventry over the winter while Barber's men had been based in the city. Hewitt said, 'I did think the persons appeared to be soldiers in disguise', and the major appeared disconcerted about Hewitt's suspicions.

On returning to Coventry he interviewed John Green who said that on the night in question he and Thomas Edwards had gone to the *Hare and Squirrel* where they sat in the company of two dragoons, John Floor of Stoneleigh, and the innkeeper's servants Richard and John Spencer. Between eleven and twelve o'clock he and Thomas Edwards and John Spencer set off for Stoneleigh. They took a footpath over the fields which led towards Berkswell and while crossing a close they were suddenly attacked and robbed by persons unknown of gold half guineas, nine shillings in silver and a few halfpence; also a pocket knife and silk handkerchief. Also interviewed was John Spencer who agreed with Green saying he was robbed of a few halfpence and a shut knife, adding that when he got up Green was still on the ground. Afterwards servants from the *Hare and Squirrel* were brought in and questioned about the evening, and especially on the two dragoons who sat with the victims and were billeted in the inn. After thirty hours questioning Hewitt accepted that these men were not involved in the crime.

On the Monday morning Hewitt wrote to Major Barber requesting that he send 'Thomas Hanbury, Robert, his comrade', and two others to him to be examined. A reply came back quickly stating that because of his request the soldiers

A scene familiar to Drury, Baker and Leslie and their victims; Park James Cottage which stood close to the Hare and Squirrel.

were immediately secured. This action seems to have spooked one, Edward Drury, who immediately went to the commanding officers and said, 'Gentlemen, irons are heavy; gaol is disagreeable and therefore I declare myself the king's evidence and insist upon being carried before a magistrate to make my confession.' This he did, turning King's evidence against another dragoon, Robert Leslie, and one other person, a Coventry weaver called Moses Baker.

On the 18 March still in Warwick, Edward Drury confessed on oath:

On the Market day ... we above [Robert Leslie and Moses Baker] *agreed to go on the highway with two pistols and one dark stock* [stick]. *We met two men on horseback and stopped them. Thus I Edward Drury stopped the first and bid him deliver, or else he was a dead man, and at the same time presented my pistol, not being willing to shoot him. The farmer being resolute rode off.*

Then Leslie knocked the other man off his horse, who was stopped by Moses Baker and was robbed of about four pounds. Then we divided the money and came home about twelve at night. Last Friday night we turned out again. All three in disguise in the road to Radford. We walked that road till about twelve at night, but meeting with no success, we thought proper to take a fresh road with a design to stop some waggoner. But no sooner in the road, then we heard a number of persons on the road coming from Coventry. We went to give them a meeting ... but all being full of liquor, we could not distinguish their tongues [how many]*, therefore turned back again and got over into the fields and walked by to get a sight of them and a little after they took the foot road to go over the fields, where we gave them the meeting.*

Moses Baker stopped the first man, demanded his money. I, Edward Drury stopped the next and demanded his money, and told him he was a dead man if he did not deliver. But the man being in liquor told me I was joking with him. Not willing to shoot him I turned the pistol about and knocked him down and so did Moses Baker do the same as I did and Leslie also to the third man and robbed them of about thirty shillings. Witnessed my hand. Edward Drury.

Hewitt wrote afterwards:

being surprised at my orders not being obeyed in sending over the men and fearful of the proceedings at Warwick, the whole discovery might be defeated. Drury's confession, from an error in the justice, being taken upon oath, and thereby rendered useless. I again sent over for their being brought before me.

After some confusion over who should prosecute, the event having apparently taken place both in the county of Coventry and Warwick, the men were eventually sent to Coventry.
    Hewitt later wrote:

I took no notice of that confession [Drury's]*, and Baker's was the first confession I took. Drury had conceived an opinion that upon a confession he should be able to clear himself, by discovering two* *of his accomplices. This is agreeable to law in cases of felony, but not in murder. This proved him a most accomplished rogue.*

Hewitt dragged Moses Baker from his bed at three in the morning and examined him for several hours before getting his confession. Baker said that he had first met Leslie when he was billeted at his house in Spon Street and at the same time Drury lay at 'Cornbill's' in Spon End. Within a short time of meeting them he became aware they were stealing geese, sheep, etc, and they soon asked Baker if he would come on the 'highway' with them, claiming they had done it before when in Kilmarnock. Hewitt was right.

Baker went out with the men for the first time and, with loaded pistols, they robbed two men on the road between Coventry and Warwick. He then claimed that on the night of the Edwards incident they were arguing after they first came across the men in the fields, and that he did not want to get near for fear of being recognized. But both Drury and Leslie told him to black his face so he would not be identified. All three then covered their faces with mud, this being verified subsequently by Drury. Contrary to Drury's original confession, Baker said that Leslie attacked the first man, Drury the second and he the last. He took the money from their pockets and Edwards ran off into the highway. Baker claimed that the two pistols belonged to Leslie; one pistol had the stock broken from the barrel and the other lost its lock and ramrod. These, Baker said, Leslie put in his boots and delivered them into the stores on the following morning and took out Drury's before the march to Warwick.

Drury was examined again and stuck to his original story followed by Robert Leslie who claimed on that night the three men in the Windmill Fields behind Spon End took off their coats and left them hidden in a sack and went off looking unsuccessfully for victims on the Radford Road. They returned via the *Hare and Squirrel* and there heard a group of noisy drinkers who would later reappear as they were ahead on the road. They left the road and Drury insisted that they attack them in the middle of a field, he states, 'Moses Baker with one loaded pistol, attacked one man, Drury with another loaded

Part of Drury, Baker and Leslie's stalking ground, Windmill Fields and Barrs Hill in the eighteenth century.

pistol, attacked another,' and Leslie claimed he attacked the third with the stick.

Leslie continued:

> *Moses Baker having done with the man ... came up to this examinant* [Leslie] *and asked what he was about? And this examinant said he could not get the money out of his pocket, upon which ... Moses Baker, struck the said person ... six or more violent blows on the head with the butt end of the pistol, upon which the man immediately dropped and this examinant really believes was the unfortunate man who is since dead and that the said wounds occasioned his death.*

Leslie then claimed the three men sat under the hedge and noted that the pistols were badly damaged; pistols Leslie now claimed belonged to Drury. After a short time he claimed two of the men got up, but did not see the man who had been struck by Moses Baker rise at all.

It appears that both soldiers, who had known each other criminally for some time, were squarely putting the blame on the weaver, Moses Baker, both claiming Baker attacked first and Leslie blaming the actual murder on Baker. Baker's belief that the pistols were Leslie's was true, despite the fact that Leslie denied it. One of the pistols was subsequently found during a search conducted after Leslie's wife was seen to hide something in the roof tiles of a privy. As the pistols were Leslie's it seems unlikely that on the night of the attack Leslie was carrying a stick as he claimed and Baker a pistol, Leslie's pistol. One cannot imagine a soldier handing his pistol to a civilian while he carried a stick.

All in all the truth of the murder of Thomas Edwards lies within the statements of these men. One of them administered the fatal blows that brought Edwards' life to a premature end. The three were eventually taken to Warwick to be tried for murder because the actual death of Edwards took place in the county of Warwick although the attack took place in the County of Coventry. Hewitt writes:

after their removal to Warwick, a strange and sudden change of conduct took place, and although they had not only to myself but to others acknowledged the favours I had shown them, as well as the indulgencies received from the gaoler through me. Instigated by the rascally and false insinuations of some persons, they not only denied what they before said, but declared they should die in peace after having blown my brains out. Such have been the returns I have always met with from men of invidious and mean principles.

Lord Leigh had already given permission, eight days before the trial, for the errection of a gibbet for the men's execution on Gallow Hill. At the end of the trial in sentencing the three men to death the judge passed on the good news saying that he was pleased to inform them that they would not be dissected by surgeons, they would instead, 'be hung in chains on Stoneleigh Common, above Wenbury Wood, by the Three Mile Stone'.

Six days later after eating breakfast, the three men left Warwick gaol sitting in an open cart and were trundled in the

Gibbet Hill as it is today. The site of the gibbet was on the right in the area now covered by trees.

pouring rain towards the Gallow Hill on Stoneleigh Common. The procession, led by twenty-four men carrying javelins, soon arrived at the newly built gallows set within a sea of thousands of people. In many ways this was no ordinary execution for it was feared the Scots Greys stationed in Coventry would try to stop it (soldiers being normally shot). To avoid this possibility the soldiers were kept out of the way by being reviewed in Coventry Park.

Another rumour, which was in circulation amongst the masses, was that a local wise woman had prophesied that if a hare ran from below the gallows a reprieve would be on the way. At twelve o'clock the three stood at their respective ladders, which would take them up the gibbet. During this time they acknowledged their guilt and even apologized for their crime to Hewitt, which apology he graciously accepted. Meanwhile Drury noticed the hangman having difficulty with his noose and offered to tie it himself, an offer the surprised hangman turned down.

Before climbing the ladders the three shook hands and kissed each other, they then climbed and the hangman placed the nooses and tied their hands. As he was doing this a great noise arose in the huge crowd as a hare burst forth from below the gibbet. The men stood perched between life and death, the

An eighteenth-century trial.

execution was stopped and a horseman sent to check if any reprieve was forthcoming. It was not, however, to be and the ladders were pulled from under the men leaving them dancing in the air, slowly choking to death.

Later the bodies were taken down, tarred and clothed in suits of metal and then rehung on the gibbet a sign to warn others who would commit such a heinous crime. The gibbet with its horrible burden stood just below the junction of the Kenilworth and Stoneleigh roads for forty-five years before the remains of the men, what little was left of them was removed. The gibbet itself leaning with a rusty chain still stood in 1822. It was finally taken down later in the nineteenth century, some

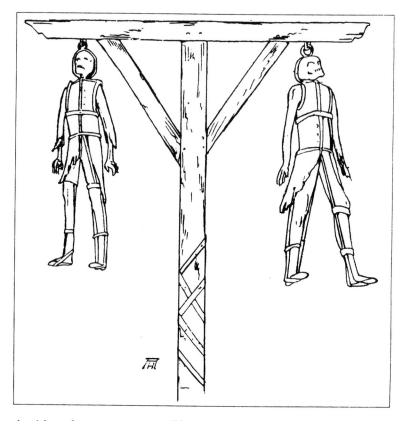

An eighteenth-century two-man gibbet.

parts being made into grisly souvenirs, while the main frame was converted into a hayrick frame at a nearby farm. It was claimed for years afterwards that the gibbet site was haunted, and the gibbet itself became a landmark burning its presence into the minds of locals. The old Gallow Hill, which had served as a gallows site in, or before the sixteenth century became the familiar Gibbet Hill, we know today.

CHAPTER 9

Murder at the Toll Gate
1772

The journal of Alderman John Hewitt records:

On the third of November [1772], information being brought to me of the Toll-gate house near Bindley [Binley] being broke into, and the gate-keeper dangerously wounded and robbed of all his cash. I directly advised the printing of some handbills for the information of the public and discovering the offenders. It being a dark night and about one in the morning, it was not possible to discern the features, but the reflexion of the fire gave him an opportunity of seeing the villain, who entered the house, so far as to be able to see his dress and to discover the colour of his hair. The other who stood behind the house at a little distance, and who spoke to his companion, his voice he very well knew was the voice of a person whom he had often discoursed with, but he could not recollect.

Within days Lord Craven of Coombe Abbey sent Hewitt a list of three suspects, but before interviewing them Hewitt went to Binley toll gate to speak to the keeper, Charles Pinchbeck, who was by that time in a serious condition. All Pinchbeck could tell him was that on the night in question possibly three men had come to the toll gate and by force broke in, and one with dark complexion, dark hair and wearing a waggoner's smock discharged a pistol which blasted through Pinchbeck's left hand. They then ransacked his house taking over nine pounds. Pinchbeck died the day after being interviewed by Hewitt.

Lord Craven's three suspects were immediately taken but were proved to be unconnected with the incident. Hewitt then arrested Thomas Farn, John Howe and John Tuckey on the grounds that

Against Farn and Howe, the first ground of the cause of suspicion, made a deep and immoveable impression on my mind; but with respect to Tuckey, his bad character and also his living in the neighbourhood of the others, were the reasons of suspecting him as the third person.

After being interviewed Tuckey confessed to another crime and also to deserting the marines so Hewitt had him committed to the assizes.

Hewitt began to interview Farn and Howe. Howe confirmed that he had been in Coventry that night, had had a drink with Farn at the *Three Horse Shoes*, left Farn to return home and passed through the toll gate arriving home at Brinklow between one and two in the morning. Farn verified that he saw Howe at the *Horse Shoes* then left him, and claimed to have gone alone down the Whitley Road to the *Back Dog Inn* and finally arrived home at Church Lawford at one the following morning.

At this point Hewitt was struck down with gout and the men were released. It was not until nearly a month later, on 28 December, he had them re-arrested along with Robert Verity. Hewitt was still weak from his illness, however, and because of lack of evidence was once again obliged to release the men. This time, however, he would have them watched.

Shortly afterwards Lord Craven offered £50 for the discovery of the offenders, then another £30 was added and Hewitt claimed that he received a threatening letter in the following post which asked

Hewitt received a threatening letter telling him to leave the stick at the base of the Coventry Cross.

him to leave the stick found at the murder scene at the base of Coventry Cross or else. Then an anonymous letter arrived stating that:

> *they are afraid as a young child is of the rod ... One of the men's wives says, if John Howe, Tom Farn and Bob Verity holds together the devil could not find it out. They are afraid every night as they go to bed, for fear anybody should come for them. This their wives themselves tell about the town ... they hardly ever work ... John Howe does nothing ... nor Bob Verity and Tom Farn of Church Lawford does nothing at all, and can buy anything, what he has a mind of, both in eating drinking and wearing apparel. All the world is in amazement how they do it, for people that work cannot do it at all ... one of the men's wives laughs about that letter that was sent to your honour and desired you to resign the stick up ...*

A few days later Hewitt received a second anonymous letter it said:

> *I take it upon me to let you know that you was wrong to release John Howe and Thomas Farn, for that Sunday that Thomas Farn was taken, John Howe's sister that lives at Coventry came post hast to our town, Brinklow ... and those that watched saw it all, and heard some of the discourse. Howe said to his sister, have they got Farn! She said yes. He then swore a great oath and said then I must go, for I am afraid he will do for me and looked as wild as he could look ... They are the two men as sure as can be I believe.*

The letter writer clearly had no love for Farn's wife for she is referred to as 'as great a bellowing bitch as any in England, or anywhere else'. A third letter arrived verifying the above and also accusing the men of robbing other places such as the Brinklow toll gate, and claimed: 'They where drinking all one day so made the poor man drunk, and at night, like rouges they robbed him, the toll-man will never think no otherways ever while he lives, but they were the men.' The letter ends, 'Pray Sir, do not let this writing be shown to anyone, pray take it off this paper, for should it be known by our town's people, they would perhaps do me some injury.'

Being distracted briefly while he secured the conviction of John Hawkins, alias Yellow Jack and his gang, Hewitt wrote:

finding myself so recovered from the painful illness which had confined me since the latter end of November, I ventured in a post chaise to Brinklow in order to examine into the robberies this notorious gang of murderers and housebreakers, had committed there ... particularly the breaking into the toll gate house ... The information's I had sent me by anonymous letters had hinted suspicion of several robberies besides the toll gate house ... and likewise the stick, which was a very remarkable one, that was left by Farn in the garden by the toll gate house ... likewise a piece of paper, which had been made use of in charging of the pistol, and which was found under the shutter, through which the fire at poor old Charles had been made ... I found upon it the name of Worcester, which gave me some reason to suspect the powder or shot had been purchased at the house of Mr. Worcester, the end of Much Park Street ... I likewise had intelligence that a person had seen, the same night the murder was committed, Thomas Farn in town, with the same stick, carrying a flag basket over his shoulder ... and he had a smock frock.

Hewitt also commented on the fact that since he issued a description of the smock Farn had stopped wearing it and the familiar stick he was known to carry was no longer to be seen.

By the 4 April 1773 Hewitt, finding himself happy with the evidence, had Farn, Howe and Verity arrested for the third time. He said:

On Farn being brought before me the next day, upon my mentioning some very strong circumstances, and which I knew were true, though he most solemnly denied his guilt ... he suddenly dropped upon the floor, as if shot through his heart. I ordered him to be taken out of the room, and upon his recovery, repeated what I had before charged ... but he denied the whole, pretending his swooning was from being brought out without his breakfast ... I had inquiry made of the gaoler ... who sent word that he never saw any man eat a more hearty breakfast ...

Hewitt found himself embarrassed because evidence was being withheld due to the interference of an unnamed clergyman and his wife. This apparently led to the release of Robert Verity who Hewitt said had the 'great insolence' to threaten him with an action for arresting him. Verity returned to Brinklow and had the bells rung in the church by way of triumph. However, with much satisfaction Hewitt adds, 'before the ringers had finished their peals, he was again apprehended upon a new warrant, granted from me that morning and brought back to Coventry'.

On that same Sunday Farn asked to see Hewitt and once again claimed that he had simply been out that night for a drink and a roast beef dinner. He did not sign this confession. That same night he was before Hewitt again and this time began to talk while Hewitt had it written down:

that he and John Howe left Coventry about eleven o'clock on the third of November last, at night. That on that day, this examinant bought below the cross, a pound of gunpowder. That Robert Verity and the said John Howe ... met him in some grounds near Newnham, and in company together wanted him to go to Coventry in order to meet some butchers as they came to the fair, in order to rob them, but which he refused to do ... some time before this they had proposed to this examinant to rob Charles Pinchbeck ... but never made the attack till the night of Coventry fair day, when he having provided shot which was bought at Worcester's ... and the said Howe set out on horseback, and this examinant on foot, till they got to the other side of Stoke, when he got up behind Howe and rode through the toll gate, up to near Bindley, when they dismounted.

John Howe said, 'We will now nail old Charles,' which this examinant did then refuse, but Howe swore by God he would and then they both proceeded to the toll gate house and took the glass light out ... he got into the room but could not get farther, and there being more people coming through the gate. Howe desired to come out till they were gone, which he did, as he could not get through the room, and then went to the front of the house, and took a pane of glass out of the casement next to the gate, when being heard Charles Pinchbeck, who called out to know what they

Binley Toll Gate as it appeared in the early twenthieth century. Celia Gilbert/David McGrory Collection

wanted ... and Charles pushed to the window shutter, and then the pistol went off ... Howe said, if he the said Charles Pinchbeck would deliver his money, he would not hurt him ... Charles gave Howe part of the money ... upon which Howe said he knew he had more, and if he would not give it to him he would fire again ... upon which Charles opened the door and let him in. Then Charles gave Howe more money ... fifty shillings ... and then they set off for Brinklow.

In his confession Farn claimed that this was not the first time Howe had robbed the toll gate, stating that the night before Whitsuntide Howe had removed a pane of glass and made an entry stealing a box containing items of clothing and over ten guineas in gold, which they spilt between them. Farn also confessed to accompanying Howe and Verity to a farm at Bilton and robbing it by force. The illiterate Farn who signed his confession with a cross also claimed Verity was involved in the toll gate robbery. He added later that the pistol used by Howe actually belonged to him and now lay in a pit in the grounds of Mr Enoch at Church Lawford. The powder used was bought from a shop below the cross in Coventry and the shot as Hewitt suspected was bought at Worcester's shop. Farn's confessions continued implicating Howe into dozens of robberies of various items from chickens to fowling guns.

When John Howe was examined subsequently he turned the tables on Farn by claiming it was Farn who said, 'Now we will have old Charles,' to which Howe claimed he replied that he would have nothing to do with it for surely Pinchbeck would recognize him. Howe claimed that once they were over Binley Bridge, 'Farn said we will get down, I have got my smock frock which I will put on and Charles wont know me … but this examinant said he would not go back, but Farn persisted and they both alighted from the horse.'

Howe then said Farn tested the pistol by putting powder in the pan and firing it, he then loaded it and they walked back to the toll-house where, Howe said, Farn removed the windowpane. Then while in the house people passed by and Howe claimed he called to Farn telling him to get out but Farn did not come out until they had passed saying him could not get through the house. He then removed a pane from the window near where Pinchbeck slept and hearing this Pinchbeck confronted him and the pistol went off. This happened Howe claimed while he stood some distance away from the toll-house wanting nothing to do with the robbery.

According to Howe he then ran up to Farn saying, 'Lord have mercy upon me, what are you at.' Pinchbeck cried out in pain and Farn shouted, 'I will have your money!' Charles he claimed gave him some halfpence from his hat and Farn said, 'This is not all the money you have, and if you wont let me in I'll shoot you again.' Farn was let in and left money in hand.

This confession is of course the reverse of Farn's, as Farn claimed Howe did the deed while Howe now claimed it was in fact Farn who did it. Who actually shot Charles Pinchbeck we may never know for sure, but I would guess it was Farn for Howe knew Pinchbeck well and claimed that during most of the robbery he stood away from the toll-house occasionally calling out. Pinchbeck himself confirmed this before his death stating that one of the men stood well away and his voice sounded very familiar having often discoursed with him. This was true for the two men were well acquainted years before when Howe worked for the Turnpike Trust that laid and maintained that road. Also Pinchbeck remembered his assailant wore a smock frock and a witness when questioned said that on that night in Coventry Farn had his smock frock with him.

It seems likely that Farn actually murdered Charles Pinchbeck, but as Howe was there too he was, in the eyes of the law, equally responsible. Hewitt later wrote:

> *Howe and Farn after a trial for six hours, were from indisputable evidence, convicted ... they were immediately sentenced to be hanged and anatomised, and which was accordingly executed upon them August 2nd 1773. A gallows was erected on a common, in the parish of Stoke, and near to the tollgate house where the robbery and murder was committed. In their last moments acknowledging all the facts charged upon them, but upon seeing Thomas Wyat [a notorious poacher] attending their execution were exceedingly disturbed ... they charged him as being the first cause of their unhappy course of life ... that he had persuaded and solicited them to obtain and get hares.*

Wyat had been the fence for much of the men's goods, but he was also in Hewitt's pocket informing on villains and indeed testifying against Farn and Howe the men whose criminal careers he had started.

As there was no evidence to implicate John Verity in the toll gate robbery he was removed to Warwick and where he stood trial for robbing the home of John Bennitt of Bilton. He received sentence of death, which was later changed to transportation for life. Hewitt concludes this entry in his journal with these words:

> *The convicting of capital offenders was the principal object of these proceedings, which have been attended with unremitting pains for near nine months, and at great charge and expence,*
> *without any government allowance whatsoever, and during six months of that time, I was confined mostly to my chamber by a most painful disorder and weak state of health.*

Farn and Howe were hung on common ground above the tollgate.
Coventry City Libraries, Local Studies

CHAPTER 10

Getting Away with Murder: The Murders of Newbold and Harris 1779

In his journal Alderman John Hewitt Junior records that:

In the morning of the 29th March [1779] I was applied to by Mr. Loynes of Corley, upon a complaint of a violent assault and abuse received by him and his neighbours from a party of soldiers belonging to the Sixth, or Warwickshire Regiment of Foot, quartered in this city ...

Hewitt interviewed all those involved in the incident. First John Barton who said that he had been detained late in Coventry on business and then picked up his horse from the *Crane Inn* in Bishopgate Street (Bishop Street) around two in the morning. The inn's ostler hung the horse's bridle on the stable door and as he did this a soldier named Samuel Hill appeared saying he would take the horse which he did and rode away towards Radford, then turned back and went down Bishop Street.

Barton, who was unwilling to tackle the soldier, sent the ostler who took his stick to retrieve the horse and as he returned back

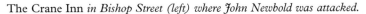

The Crane Inn *in Bishop Street (left) where John Newbold was attacked.*

to the inn another local Keresley farmer, John Newbold, who had just picked up his horse from the *Anchor* arrived immediately before fellow farmer Thomas Loynes and enquired as to what was the problem. At this moment another soldier James Manley grabbed the harness of Mr Newbold's horse. Newbold told him to loose the animal, but the soldier replied 'damn you and your horse too.' Newbold struck out at the soldier, then struck his horse to make it move off, but Manley, now joined by other soldiers dragged him off the horse down onto the ground.

John Hunter of the *Crane Inn* testified that during the attack on Newbold he witnessed that James Manley drew out his bayonet, but he did not see him use it. But Hewitt sent an order to the commanding officer of the troops stationed in Coventry informing him of the assault and adding that during the attack, 'Newbold hath received two dangerous stabs and his recovery very doubtful.'

Manley was examined and stated he had been on duty at the barn guard house, near the navigation yard (canal basin) and he and some other soldiers had gone down to the *Crane* to ask Mr Hunter for some beer, Hunter refused. He then claimed that he returned a second time only to witness some gentlemen quarrelling but ignored it and returned to his sentry box.

Manley then continued that while he was standing at his box those same gentlemen approached him on horseback and one, Newbold, came up to him and said, 'Damn your blood. I will leather everyone who wears the cloth.' He then struck him twice, whereupon when he dismounted Manley stated that he put his bayonet to his breast and told him to go about his business. He then claimed another soldier helped him back on his horse and Newbold apologized for insulting them. As will be seen, this was mostly a lie. Samuel Flint the corporal in command that night was also less than

An eighteenth-century foot soldier.

forthcoming, and claimed that he placed Manley on duty at two and never saw or heard anything else that night.

However, on 29 March Hewitt wrote to Colonel Cane requiring him to bring forward another soldier, 'to be examined touching the murder of John Newbold'. Newbold was not in fact dead at that point but there was no hope for recovery. Samuel Gilbert did not witness the event, but said that, 'when he went to the guardhouse, Price told him that Manley had stabbed a man in two places, that morning between one and two o'clock'.

Farmer Newbold died on 30 March and Hewitt again wrote to Colonel Cane calling for Patrick MacDonald, a gunner in the regiment, for examination. He was questioned two days later and Hewitt said that on that night MacDonald saw many of the soldiers, including Manley, drinking at the *Nag's Head* by the canal basin. A group of the soldiers went back to the guardhouse but when they reached the gate Manley violently stopped them by drawing his bayonet and attempting to stab MacDonald.

James Chalmers of the *Nag's Head* told Hewitt that when he arrived at the scene the incident had passed and he saw John Newbold leaning against his saddle groaning, and two of the soldiers, Price and MacDonald, helped him back onto his horse and he left the scene, bloodied, with the other farmers.

To finally pin down Manley, Hewitt also interviewed one Benjamin Icliff and wrote:

> *being on Saturday morning last at the gate at the navigation yard, having before heard of John Newbold being stabbed with a bayonet that morning by one Manley, a soldier and seeing Manley then on duty at the guard yard gate he said to Manley, 'Was not you a villain to stab a man in that manner?' Upon which Manley answered, 'Damn you, you are an American and I will take my bayonet and run it up to the hilt', and continued to say 'I did prick him and meant to prick him', meaning John Newbold.*

Following the inquest into John Newbold's death a charge of murder was laid against Manley and three other soldiers. Hewitt wanted a full prosecution and attempted to persuade Newbold's fellow farmers to prosecute for murder. However, fearing for their own safety the men refused. By that time the troopers had left Coventry and Hewitt sent for Thomas Newbold, brother of the victim, and bound him over to prosecute or face a penalty of £100. Thomas Newbold not surprisingly agreed.

At this point Hewitt again falls victim to his problem, which he describes as a, 'fluctuating gouty disorder.' That, with a slow fever, prevented him from personally pursuing the case and he passed his notes on to an attorney. He concludes:

I wrote to the secretary of State and the Secretary of war to desire Flint, & co. who were then in camp … to attend the trial … the soldiers were in court accordingly, but whether called, or not, I do not know, nor to this day for what reasons the inhuman Manley, and his accomplices were acquitted and discharged without punishment.

Hewitt also dealt with a second murder at this time, November 1779, that of William Harris a herdsman and pinner who was employed by the city chamberlains to herd and pin stray cattle on the Michaelmas and Lammas Lands. It is thought that Harris may have recently impounded some cattle or horses belonging to one James Draycot. While having a drink in an unspecified inn on that snowy November night Harris was confronted by Draycot who pushed him in the chest and, 'damned him for a rouge'.

Then, as a witness Richard Clarke swore,

Draycot damned Harris [again] and said he would roll him in the snow, and they agreed to go out. Harris was standing all this time and upon Draycot's rising there were blows immediately struck and Harris dropped on the bench, when Draycot struck him twice, and then Harris fell to the ground and much blood fell from his nose … Harris when he was on the bench, never spoke, and appeared to be then dead, and then Draycot struck him again, he then dropped to the ground and although apparently dead, Draycot again struck him upon the temples.

During this vicious attack no one saw Harris strike a single blow.

Hewitt had Draycot taken and committed for trial, which he was too ill to attend; however, James Draycot was acquitted of murder.

CHAPTER 11

The Kenilworth Road Murder
1818

Unlike most of the events in this book this crime has a modern feel about it, a typical piece of modern thuggery, although taking place in 1818. It was reported in the *Coventry Mercury* on 28 September 1818:

On Thursday last, an inquisition was taken before Mr. Carter, Coroner for this City and County at the Windmill public house at Stivichall, near this City, on view of the body of William Law (aged 25) who met with his death under the following circumstances.

On Tuesday last, a young man of the name of Jacob Moore, of this City in company with Thomas Wickes, William Bird and another were going from Coventry to Kenilworth, between 8 and 9 o'clock in the evening. Within about three quarters of a mile of Kenilworth they were met by William Jackson (aged 21) and several other young men and women.

As Moore and his party were passing them, someone cried out, 'Our side go the rig,' and suddenly, Moore and his companions were knocked down and beaten very severely. William Bird lost his hat in the affray.

Within a few minutes, another young man, Joseph Bird, came up to them and told them that he too had been attacked by the group. He said he would go back to Kenilworth, where there were several other Coventry persons and bring them so they could give each other protection.

Joseph Bird soon returned with his companions, who were all fired up and decided they would go after the individuals and regain Bird's stolen hat. The press continues:

They overtook them on Gibbet Hill, where Jackson or one of his party was kicking out the light of a man who had stationed

The Kenilworth Road today looking towards Gibbet Hill. The attack on Law took place 100 yards below the summit.

himself there with refreshments for the persons returning from Kenilworth Statues.

Here William Law, the deceased came up to them in company with a young man named Turner, on his return from the Statues. An enquiry was made from the Coventry party for the hat, which had been lost, and they denied having it. Both parties proceeded down the hill towards Coventry and about 100 yards from the summit, the same person who had given the signal when Moore and his companions were assaulted, again cried out, 'Our side go rig.'

A fight immediately began with sticks, &c., which lasted a short time, on which several were severely beaten and they proceeded a little farther, when a second attack commenced. The deceased (Law), (who appeared particularly opposed in the quarrel to a man named Carpenter, one of Jackson's party), here was heard to cry out, 'I'll fight him, if he will show fair play.' Jackson immediately jumped between them with a stick in his hand and became the antagonist of Law.

At this moment another young man, James Bird, who had run back a considerable distance, on hearing the noise, came up to Law and asked what he was about. Law replied, 'The man

(Jackson) is going to kill me with his stick and I'll take it from him.' Shortly afterwards Law seized an opportunity, ran in upon Jackson and after a short struggle wrenched the stick out of his hands. This happened in the middle of the road. Someone here cried out from near the footpath, 'D— him, pull your knife out and stick it in him.'

Jackson immediately pulled out a knife and began to flourish it about, swearing most dreadfully that he would stick it into the first man that came near him. He was requested by a young man named Walker to put it up, but he swore that he would put it into him if he did not keep off.

Jackson then began to approach Law with the knife and Law retreated towards a hedge followed by Jackson. Jackson made a thrust at Law and Law struck him on the shoulder with the stick. Jackson again thrust at Law who this time struck him hard enough to bring him to his knees. Jackson, however, sprang back to his feet and as James Bird grabbed Law, Jackson rushed forward thrusting his knife fully into Law's stomach. He then stepped back and said, 'How do you like that.'

Law is reported to have responded with the words, 'Oh dear! He has stabbed me, my bowels are coming out.' This exclamation may well have been adapted by the press who tended not to publish swear words, and had earlier avoided printing the word, 'damn'.

Jackson and Carpenter ran off pursued by some of those present at the attack, and both ran past the *Windmill* but were finally caught, exhausted, a short distance away at the Stivichall toll gate. While he was running Jackson threw the knife into undergrowth, it was never recovered and possibly it still lies there to this day. A cart was procured on which William Law was carried in agony down the Kenilworth Road to the *Windmill* pub. Here surgeons were called and they were obliged to enlarge the wound so they could re-insert Law's intestines.

Law lay at the Windmill in agonizing pain all night until 9 am the following morning when he died. A two-day inquest ended with a verdict of wilful murder against Jackson, who was

The Windmill Inn, *Stivichall, known locally as the* White House *because it was painted white. Here William Law died and his inquest was held.* Coventry City Libraries, Local Studies

detained in Coventry gaol until he stood trial at Warwick, probably because the actual stabbing took place just outside the County of Coventry and within the County of Warwick. He was found guilty of manslaughter, although details of his sentence remain uncertain.

CHAPTER 12

The Sensational Golsby Murder
1844

Perhaps one of Coventry's most sensational murder trials was that of thirteen-year-old Susannah Jarvis for the murder of Emma Golsby aged just seventeen months in August 1844. Two days after the murder an inquest was held before a jury of fourteen at the *Wheel Tavern* in Leicester Row. From this eight-hour inquest the following evidence was put forth:

It appeared that on Monday evening last the only persons at home at the Canal Tavern, were Mrs Golsby and her children, namely Ann, aged 9 years, Mary, aged 4 years and the deceased infant Emma, aged 17 months; together with nurse-girl, Susannah Jarvis, aged under 13 years, who was brought before the jury in custody on suspicion of having committed the murder.

Between seven and eight o'clock, Mrs Golsby having laid the infant in the cradle, which stood in the back kitchen went up stairs with the child Mary, to take it to bed, leaving the nurse-girl in the back kitchen to mind the babe; and her daughter Ann in charge of the bar. After being up stairs a minute or two Mrs Golsby heard a cry of anguish or distress, which she could scarcely describe, and she called out, 'What is the matter?' to

Leicester Row or Causeway site of the Canal Tavern. Coventry City Libraries, Local Studies

which enquiry receiving no answer, she immediately ran downstairs; but before she arrived at the bottom, the cry had ceased, and Jarvis called out to her, 'A man has killed, or a man has stabbed the baby!'

Mrs Golsby then rushed from the stairs to the back kitchen, and as she was entering, met Jarvis coming out, somewhat agitated and rubbing her hands together on some part of her dress, or pinafore, when the latter repeated, 'A man has killed, or stabbed the baby, and has run down the yard.' On going to the cradle she found her infant suffused with blood about the head and bosom, and taking it up, she fled with it, horror stricken to the front door, and cried out murder.

Several persons immediately came in and the child was passed from the mother into other hands, and after a few gasping breaths expired. Not more than four minutes had elapsed from the time of Mrs. Golsby going up stairs, to her coming down again ...

The inquest was then told that on the Monday before the murder Mrs Golsby had written to Susannah Jarvis's parents in Kenilworth, informing them that as the child no longer liked its young nurse as much as it had when Susannah had started at Michaelmas, she intended to send Susannah home, but may try her another week. Apparently the message was read out to Susannah by her parents so she knew that her position was at risk.

The inquest report adds significantly:

The child had never been fond of her from the first, but had latterly shown great aversion towards her. Mrs Golsby, however said that she had never known the girl to beat the child. She shook it once soon after she came, but having been scolded for it, had not been known to do so since ... Last Friday evening, about six o'clock, Mrs. Golsby wiped her infant's face and neck, and gave it to the nurse-girl to take a walk. There were then no marks such as scratches or bruises of any kind about it. She returned about seven and undressed the child and put it in the cradle to sleep. Shortly afterwards, Mrs. Golsby heard it break into a sharp and sudden cry. On going to it she observed upon its neck, several marks, as if produced by pinching, or scratching of fingernails, but the skin was not broken.

Angrily questioned about this, Jarvis swore no one had touched the child while they were out and she certainly had not.

Jarvis certainly appeared to be the culprit, however, for on the following day the child refused to be left with her and Mrs Golsby had another servant take care of her. When 9-year-old Ann was questioned she said she was minding the bar, and as to a stranger stabbing the baby, she declared no one could have entered the front or back of the building without her seeing them. Mr Overton, the surgeon, then testified and said the child had been stabbed with a carving knife, which had been found, bloodstained at the scene, and which had come from a box on the dresser next to the cradle. The knife had cut the jugular vein and almost passed through the back of the child obliquely between its ribs.

Police Constable Salmon stated that Jarvis was called and in the presence of him and Mr Overton said suddenly, 'I am sure it was not me that did it; look at my hands, how clean they are.' This statement she soon after repeated. The appropriately named Police Inspector Vice took Jarvis into custody later that evening and advised her not to say anything, unless she wished to voluntarily make a statement. This brought forth a story not mentioned earlier that day to the effect that she claimed that when her mistress had gone upstairs, she left the child to go to the outside privy and on returning saw a man with blood on his hands (later she would say blood on his feet) coming from the direction of the back door and going past the stable. She said he was a tall man, walking barefooted and she would not recognize him if she saw him again.

Vice added that he had checked the girl's hands earlier and they were clean, then Chief Constable Prosser on being called produced the clothes Jarvis had worn earlier and pointed out that four spots of blood were distinctly visible on the bosom of the pinafore and the middle part was discoloured with a reddish hue (as one would find if someone had rubbed their bloody hands clean). On the bottom of the frock were a dozen spots of blood. Jarvis then claimed that the marks on the pinafore were made when she leaned on the dresser and those on her frock from when she fell in the passage. It was noted however that the spots did not correspond with leaning or falling and also both areas were clear of blood, except for a spot where the knife lay on the dresser, which lay undisturbed. The press observed that on this first night, 'The conduct of the prisoner ... we were pained to observe was far from becoming. She is thin, and rather agreeable, sharp looking country girl; but her demeanour on this occasion evinced a trifling indifference, and almost pertness ...'

Everything looked clear cut, but on the second evening of the inquest a woman named Watts from Tower Street, was called and said that after hearing the girl's statement about a barefooted man she had recollected that on the night in question at about seven she saw a man in Leicester Street without shoes going towards the *Cottage* public house. She did not watch him continuously but stated that he was within one hundred yards of the back way to the *Canal Tavern*. She then said in contradiction to Jarvis that the man was short and stooped at the shoulders.

Thomas King, also a resident of Tower Street was also questioned and added that on coming down the Radford Road on Monday night at about eight thirty he saw a man sitting on a bank by the side of a field, near the residence of the Reverend Mr Howells. The man wore no shoes and was staring intently at something cupped in his hands. Certain points of law were then cleared with the jury and in half-an-hour a verdict of wilful murder was brought against Susannah Jarvis. She received this announcement calmly, but she told her mother who was crying not to mind for she had not done anything. She was then sentenced to be put on trial for murder.

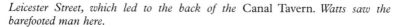

Leicester Street, which led to the back of the Canal Tavern. *Watts saw the barefooted man here.*

The trial took place on Tuesday, 6 August 1844 before Mr Justice Coltman at the County Hall. It is said that the court was filled with, a 'large assemblage of spectators, chiefly of a highly respectable and well-dressed class of person.' The trial was much like the inquest except that the bare-footed man had been identified and was called up. He was described as a 'miserable fiddler' from Foleshill, and he appeared to be unsure whether his name was Jones or Davis, although he was well known to the magistrates under both names as a drunk.

Witnesses were now brought forward who saw the man in the street a number of times that afternoon and even saw him leaving the back entrance to the *Canal Tavern*. These witnesses did, however, all agree that it was not at the time of the murder that he was seen. Apparently Jones or Davis was in the habit of searching for food, one witness saw him pick up some orange peel off the road and eat it. Probably on his route home he was in the habit of popping round to the back of the *Canal Tavern* in search of scraps, and perhaps Susannah Jarvis knew this.

The only people to stand up for Jarvis was the Reverend Mr Parry of Kenilworth and the schoolmistress who swore that she was a kind-hearted girl. Summing up, the judge informed the jury of the law relating to children between the ages of seven and fourteen, saying that their responsibility was usually determined by the degree of the child's intelligence. Under those circumstances Jarvis could be found guilty because she was considered to be intelligent. It was also pointed out that the 'fiddler' was not at the scene at the time of the murder, and even if he were, he had no motive to do such a thing.

The jury retired with the knife and plans of the house. Ten and a half hours later they requested water, but the judge turned down their request. The court closed and the jury were locked in for the night without, it was said, 'fire and candle'. At half-past six on Wednesday morning Justice Coltman visited them and ordered that bread and water be brought, this was changed to milk after a doctor gave the judge some 'medical' advice. At ten o'clock the court re-opened and the prisoner and jury returned. The clerk asked them if they had reached a verdict to which the foreman answered that they had not and could not. The judge then discharged the jury and ordered that Jarvis, who had remained calm and indifferent during the whole trial to be remanded until the next assizes.

At the second trial a detailed model of the tavern, its rooms and the surrounding streets was used, but little or nothing new was added, except that Susan Golsby now claimed that when she came down stairs and was told a man had stabbed the baby, she said, 'Where's the man gone?' and Jarvis replied, 'Down the yard,' to which Susan Golsby retorted, 'No, it's no man; it's you I doubt!' After which she picked up the child and cried, 'Murder'. She added that, 'When I picked the child up I did not perceive it to move; the prisoner never came near to it after I took it up, nor did I go near the prisoner. I was several yards off her, and told her not to come near me.'

Mr Humfrey addressed the court for the prisoner saying that the absence of motive ought not be considered immaterial

Plans issued to the jury showing the downstairs layout of the Golsby residence.

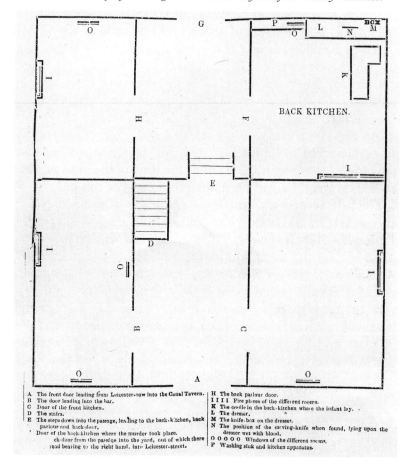

A	The front door leading from Leicester-row into the Canal Tavern.
B	The door leading into the bar.
C	Door of the front kitchen.
D	The stairs.
E	The steps down into the passage, leading to the back-kitchen, back parlour and back-door.
'	Door of the back-kitchen where the murder took place. ck-door from the passage into the yard, out of which there road bearing to the right hand, into Leicester-street.
H	The back parlour door.
I I I I	Fire places of the different rooms.
K	The cradle in the back-kitchen where the infant lay.
L	The dresser.
M	The knife-box on the dresser.
N	The position of the carving-knife when found, lying upon the dresser wet with blood.
O O O O O	Windows of the different rooms.
P	Washing sink and kitchen apparatus.

INFORMATION.

To the Registrar of Births and Deaths in the District of

Pursuant to the Act of 6 & 7 Gulielmi IV. c. 86, intituled "*An Act for Registering* "*Births, Deaths, and Marriages in England,*" I hereby inform you that at an Inquest held by me the *twenty third* day of *April* — 184 4 , in the *Parish* — of *the Holy Trinity* — *in the County of Warwick* on the Body of *Emma Goldsby* — then and there lying dead, the Jury found as follows :—

Time and Place of Death	Name and Surname	Sex	Age	Rank or Profession	Cause of Death
2nd April 44 in ester Row	Emma Goldsby	Female	18 Months	Infants Daughter of Robert and Susan Goldsby	Wound in the throat — Murder

Witness my hand this *twenty fourth* day of *April* i — 184 4 .

Wm Henry Seymour Coroner.

A surviving fragment of the original death certificate of Emma Golsby, spelt here 'Goldsby' and stating the cause of death, 'Murder'. Coventry City Libraries, Local Studies

as to evidence of guilt; he also desperately claimed that blood spots four feet high on the wall must have fallen from the knife and therefore attested that the killer when holding the knife must have been taller than Jarvis. He also reminded the jury that the previous jury had failed to reach a verdict, implying that the girl must be innocent, and added that during the previous ten months she had spent in gaol, she maintained a complete silence, showing he believed her innocence. Silence, however, can imply guilt.

The judge finally gave a lengthy summing up, referring to the tediousness of the case and despite strong evidence to the contrary argued in favour of the prisoner. His advice and thoughts were heard by the jury and they were warned that they must reach a verdict. After just twenty minutes, the verdict prompted by the judge, was reached, and Susannah Jarvis to the surprise of all those present was acquitted and walked free. The press did not record the thoughts of the dead child's mother.

CHAPTER 13

Singular Suicides

Early in January 1850, an unusual suicide took place in Spon Street. Rumours were rife in the street and surrounding district, that fifty-year-old John Bowen had been seen off by his wife and daughter-in-law. These allegations were investigated but nothing certain came to light. The inquest took place at the *Dyers Arms* in Spon Street, which was at that time under the landlordship of a Mr Walmsey. The first witness was Samuel Lines, a shoemaker who told the jury:

I live up the dark entry in Spon Street, next door to the deceased, who had resided there for five or six years, and when in health, had been in the habit of working on the railways. Yesterday morning, a little before eight o'clock, I heard his daughter-in-law cry out as if very much alarmed, 'Lines, do come in here.' I immediately lighted a candle and went in, and then found the deceased in bed, with his face downwards in a bucket of water; a rope being tied, one end to the bedpost, drawn across the back of his neck, and at the other end was fastened a brick hanging down, but not to the ground, and so as to bear his head down to the water. It was a tin bucket, somewhat above half full. His face was in the water and when I took it away it was quite wet and soddened. He was quite dead, stiff, and cold. He had been ill some time, and nearly confined to his bed, which was in the room downstairs where he now lies.

Dr Drew said Bowen had suffered from typhus fever and a bowel complaint the previous September and had recovered, but about a fortnight previously he was called to him as he was suffering a bout of dropsy. He was under treatment and getting better. Drew said:

The last time I saw him alive was on Monday. He and his wife had asked me what I thought of his case, and I told them I thought he would recover, but he would not be able to attend to his

*work during the winter ... His wife appeared attentive to him ...
He seemed a quiet reserved sort of man, and I had an impression
he was a good deal depressed in spirits. He was in a weakly state,
but certainly able to lift a bucket of water and do all he seems to
have done to take away his life.*

The next witness was Lucy Grainger who said:

*I am the daughter-in-law of the deceased ... I live in the same
house as the deceased, and slept in the room above him. He slept
in the room downstairs since he has been so poorly ... A little
before one o'clock I heard him press her [his wife] to come up
stairs to get an hour or two's sleep; and when she left him, I heard
him wish her good night, and say that if he was worse he would
call her. She never went downstairs afterwards, and I did not hear
any noise during the night. I went downstairs first thing in the
morning, a little before eight o'clock. He was in bed with his face
in a bucket, and a rope over the back of his neck ... In a regular
way since the water tap was frozen we had fetched in a bucket of
water at night, and it was set near the foot of the stairs. He was
very low spirited of late and seemed to fret very much ... I don't
know where he got the rope from ...*

The jury returned a verdict that John Bowen had committed
suicide as described, being at the time in a state of temporary
insanity. Full details of the inquest were published in the
Coventry Herald to try to dispel the continuing rumours that
Mrs Bowen and her daughter-in-law were responsible in some
way for his death.

In January 1859 an inquest was held at the *Roebuck Inn* in
Little Park Street on the body of James Knight. In this case the
surgeon who examined him found an unusual suicide note. He
told the inquest that the young man had been brought to the
hospital in Little Park Street at about 11.30 on the Thursday
night, suffering from a gunshot wound to the chest. He said:

*I saw it was mortal at the time, the stomach protruded. He lived
about fourteen to fifteen hours. He became sensible after his
admission and told me that he had done it himself. There were two*

or three shots at the edge of the wound. The stomach was injured and perhaps the lungs. I found the pocket book and paper produced in his pocket.

The pocketbook entry was read out in court, it said:

Miss Feltham, — It was my intention when I started from home to end both our lives, but I have altered my mind. I have nothing now to live for, therefore my only wish is to die near to you. I hope you will not think hard of me whatever you hear. My last breath shall be spent in blessing you, and hoping your future life will be one of usefulness. I hope you take warning from my fate,

The Roebuck, *Little Park Street, a medieval inn and scene of James Knight's inquest.* Coventry City Libraries, Local Studies

and marry the man you ought, and not make a fool of anyone else. I should have been a useful young man, had I not have loved you so much. I cannot write any more, so farewell James Knight. P.S. You are very happy now, I hope you may ever be so.

Inside the pocketbook was a piece of paper on which was written the following lines:

> *What is love? If thou would'st be taught,*
> *Thy heart must teach alone:*
> *Two minds with but a single thought*
> *Two hearts that beat as one.*
>
> *And when comes love? Like morning light*
> *It comes without thy call;*
> *Thou did'st love a spirit bright,*
> *Love never errs at all.*

The next witness in this sad affair was the father of Miss Feltham landlord of the *Plough Inn* in Spon Street. He told the inquest:

I knew the deceased. He was a weaver, and he worked for me more than seven years. His friends lived near Red Lane. I did not know that he paid his address to my daughter. He has not been at my house many times since I lived at the Plough. About twenty minutes before eleven on Thursday night, my wife, who was in the parlour, called to me to go into the tap room. When I got there he lay on his back and I thought it was a drunken man. I said he had better go home; went to turn him round and saw his clothes were on fire. He said, 'I've shot myself,' and I then saw who he was. We then sent for assistance. Mr. Barton, surgeon and Dr. Waters came. They recommended his removal to hospital.

Police Constable Jackson told the inquest, 'When I got there I found the body lying on three chairs. I asked him what he had done with the instruments he did it with. He said he had thrown it behind the fire. I looked but could not find it. I ultimately found it under the dresser.'

It was then decided to investigate Knight's state of mind immediately before his death. His brother testified to the jury:

My brother was 22 years of age and he slept with me at home. We have both been at home with nothing to do the last month. I believe he felt some regard for Miss Feltham, but I don't know that any correspondence took place between them. He has been rather stupid at times lately. When anyone has remonstrated with him lately, he has not answered. I understand he was in bed till four on Thursday without speaking to anyone.

Strangely the press did not record whether Miss Feltham, the young lady at the centre of this incident, appeared before the inquest. If she did she must have told the jury that there was nothing between her and Knight because no reason could be found for Knight to have killed himself. On that basis the judge advised the jury to find that Knight suffered a temporary state of insanity and the jury accordingly brought in the verdict, 'destroyed himself while labouring under temporary insanity'. So this was a young man who had apparently gone mad, or really was desperately in love with Miss Feltham, even though she claimed to be unaware of it, as were her father and Knight's brother. It could be that there was something going on between the couple and there was in fact another party in Miss Feltham's affections. That would explain why the note said, 'marry the man you ought, and not make a fool of anyone else'. Another odd aspect to the case is that although Knight apparently shot himself three or four times in the taproom, nobody heard it, as indeed they would have done even if he had done it in the street. Also there was his confusion concerning the whereabouts of the gun, was this simply due to his condition or was there another reason. Assuming James Knight had not gone temporarily insane there were most definitely details concerning this incident that were withheld from the inquest.

Another verdict of self-destruction during a fit of insanity had been given some twenty-six years earlier on Joseph White. His inquest was held at the *Hawthorn Tree*, next to Hearsall Common, which coincidentally was the last place he was seen alive. It appears that White was at the time lodging in Broad Lane and came into Coventry to receive, 'his pension', possibly a freeman's seniority fund payment. On his way back he often drank at the *Hawthorn* and after spending all his pension on drink informed those present on a number of occasions that he had but a few days to live.

Those who met him later that day said he often stated that the devil was sitting on him. The next morning he took his shaving razor with him and went to the *Hawthorn Tree* for a drink. What happened next was reported in the *Coventry Herald*:

> *after calling at the Hawthorn Tree, he went to the Beech Wood, where there is every reason to believe he committed suicide, the razor being found under the body. When discovered, last Saturday, his stick was standing against a tree by the body, and his hat upon it, with his neckhandkerchief in it. The head was a short distance from the body, and the flesh completely eaten from*

every part of it by vermin. He was buried on Tuesday at Stoneleigh. The jury returned a verdict, — 'That he had committed the act of self destruction in a fit of insanity.'

On Thursday, 6 July 1858 Margaret Hennessey was found hanged in the Workhouse (the old Whitefriars Monastery was converted to a workhouse in 1801). Margaret lived near the well in Well Street and about ten days previous to the tragic event her husband left for Ireland taking with him one of the children. This left her alone with five children and over the days that followed she was drinking heavily. By Tuesday morning she was in such a state that Dr Phillips visited her and found her to be, 'decidedly insane' and ordered a constable to keep her confined in the house. That night as midnight approached she got out and began screaming in a rage in the streets cursing and screaming threats to kill her children. She was taken by the city constables to the police station, and at 1.30 am on Wednesday morning was charged with being, 'disorderly in Well Street'. It was said at the time that the prisoner was obviously insane.

On Wednesday morning she appeared before the magistrates who, following Dr Phillips's advice, ordered that she be taken to the workhouse, as a 'dangerous lunatic' and be confined in a room. The following morning she was found hanging from the bedstead, which she had turned on its end for the purpose. The inquest was held in the workhouse on the Friday and Sarah Geary, described as a nurse at the Coventry Union Workhouse, told the jury:

I knew the deceased; she was brought here ... on Wednesday last. The same night about 8

Well Street as it was at the time Margaret Hennessey lived there.

o'clock she was put into a bath, and afterwards put to bed. I think her age to be about 45 years; she was singing all night, so that those within hearing could not get any rest. In the morning I was called down stairs by Mrs. Sayer (the nurse in the lunatic ward), about half-past six o'clock, who told me the deceased had hung herself. No one had gone in to see her from the time she was put to bed till she was found in the morning. When lunatics are first brought into the house they often sing for a night or two. When I was called in the morning I found the deceased hanging from the bedstead, which she had turned up on end. She had torn the sheet, and part of it she had used to suspend herself. She was quite dead when I and Sayers cut her down. I saw no froth about her mouth; her hands were clenched a little; everything was removed from the room with which it was thought possible she could destroy herself.

Police Constable Lee, who had been watching her, was the next to give evidence, saying:

I saw the deceased in the street several times naked and very violent. I also saw her up at the chamber window, holding the youngest child out of the window. Several persons advised her to come down and dress herself, she did so, and eventually I took her to the station house. I thought it my duty to do so, because I had taken a knife from her while she was on her knees praying to God and to Father Pratt to forgive her before she did any harm to her children.

At the police station she was handed over and was described as being, 'very violent' during the night. Police Constable Wood testified that she did not appear to be in drink but because of her violence they checked her every two minutes. The verdict was that Margaret Hennessy had hung herself, 'being at the time in a unsound state of mind'. The court complimented the police's handling of the incident but criticized the Union Workhouse for not watching her on the night of her death. This caused somewhat of a scandal but the workhouse was later cleared as they claimed they had not been informed of the woman's condition.

The ex-monastery cloister of Whitefriars laid out as the dining hall after the building became a workhouse.

The *Coventry Standard* noted that after the trial a certain Samuel Jennings asked for a copy of the court's evidence claiming he wanted it to be sent to the deceased's husband in Ireland. It was agreed to sell him a copy for two shillings on condition that it was used for no other purpose. Despite that promise, the particulars of the case were hawked on the streets of Coventry the next day as a penny dreadful.

An unusual footnote to this story is that some years ago the body of a woman with nineteenth-century multi-buttoned boots was seen hanging in a stairwell of the old workhouse. Those who saw her believed her real enough to consider calling the police. On returning to the scene however nothing was found. Was this Margaret Hennessey or some other unfortunate who ended her days violently in the Union Workhouse.

CHAPTER 14

Murder at the Black Dog
1854

The *Coventry Herald* of 29 April 1854 reported an incident which shook Coventry:

On Saturday evening last, between six and seven o'clock, one of the most fearful events took place in this City which has ever been recorded in its annals, and a horrifying sensation quickly became general, from the statement that a man had murdered his wife and then blown out his own brains.

The two people involved were Nelson Webb, aged twenty-two years, and his wife Eliza, aged twenty-five. They had been married for some time and had both until, shortly before the event, occupied the *Black Dog Inn* in Silver Street. The press stated that Nelson was generally considered to be a decent and rather amiable young fellow. Unfortunately,

Too soon, however, he conceived he had reason to suspect his wife's fidelity towards him, and in addition to this, his business affairs became embarrassed – evils which were further aggravated by the conviction that his wife had another husband living in America, a fact of which it had been said, Webb was aware of at the time he married her.

'Be that as it may', the press continued, 'it is not denied that he was passionately attached to her.' Because of this problem the couple's relationship was strained and Webb left the *Black Dog* after selling many of his personal effects. The licence previously in his hands was transferred to a relative of his wife called Thompson. Webb's existence was unsettled but his wife remained at the *Black Dog*.

That Friday things took a turn for the worse as Webb purchased a pistol and then bought a second pistol the following morning. It would seem then that Webb was planning to do something at that time, however, he must have had a change of heart for instead of confronting his wife he went to the police station and laid a charge of bigamy against her stating she had a husband by the name of Poole in America. The case went before the magistrates and was adjourned three times.

What happened next was reported at the inquest held at the *Holly Bush* in Cook Street. The first witness, James Hopkins of Cook Street, said:

> *about 7 o'clock in the evening of Saturday last I was in the kitchen of the house* [Black Dog] *… the deceased* [Eliza] *was in the bar close by the kitchen with a man named Thompson, her brother-in-law. Webb came in about 7 o'clock and asked his wife to let him have a glass of ale; she refused to let him have it; he told her he had money to pay for it, but she still refused to let him have anything … Webb came into the kitchen, and she followed him; he went close to her and said, 'I will shoot you', to which she replied, 'Don't be fool-hardy.' Almost immediately I heard the report of a pistol, and in less than a minute after heard a second report.*

It was stated that Hopkins ran from the inn in a panic.

When asked if Webb had also threatened to shoot him, Hopkins replied that he had not, and then continued by stating that he had never previously witnessed anything unpleasant happen between Webb and his wife before and did not know anything else about the affair.

Unimpressed, the Coroner retorted:

> *I have never heard a more confused account of any circumstances in my life; if you had possessed the least courage, you might have prevented this dreadful catastrophe, by seizing his arm and taking the pistol from him, as you admit you saw what he was about to do and certainly sufficient time had elapsed between the threat and the actual firing of the pistol to have enabled you to do so.*

Nelson Webb shoots Eliza in the Black Dog.

Hopkins continued to answer questions becoming more and more excited and unnerved until he was a gibbering wreck and was dismissed. The second witness, one Samuel Taylor, was then called. He said he was at the *Black Dog* about five o'clock and found Hopkins and Mrs Webb together in the kitchen. He recalled that Nelson Webb came in around six o'clock and asked for a glass of spirits, she refused to let him have it, he then asked her for a glass of ale, which was also refused. That took place in the front room [bar], then they both went into the kitchen and Webb pushed her against the cellar door.

Taylor stated that he heard a percussion cap go off and said to Hopkins, 'He's got a pistol,' and Hopkins replied, 'I believe he has.' It later became clear that Webb had put the pistol close to Eliza's head and fired, but only the cap went off so he replaced it and fired a second time, this time the gun worked and Eliza fell dead to the ground. Taylor then said, 'Good God, Webb, you have killed your wife,' upon which Webb turned to Taylor pointing his second pistol at him saying, 'I killed her.' Webb's hand was shaking violently and he fired, but again, the gun misfired and only the cap went off. Taylor in a panic ran from the building, taking refuge in a neighbouring building. He returned with assistance but he found Webb had shot himself, the shock of which caused him to faint.

Mr John Overton a surgeon stated to the jury that he had been called to the *Black Dog* around seven o'clock and on opening the kitchen door he found Mrs Webb lying behind it on her right side, and quite dead. On raising her head he found an

irregular wound behind the right ear ... he should say that the pistol was close to her head when it was fired. She had a newspaper in her hand, which no doubt she had raised towards her face when he was shooting at her, as it caught fire. The charge of the pistol had gone quite through her brain, there was a great discharge of blood and she must have died instantly.

James Hopkins was recalled and said that he did not hear a cap go off, nor had he had any conversation with Taylor on the subject. He said, 'I was certainly much frightened, but can't say exactly why.' A reporter said that Hopkins, was, 'either very much mystified himself, or desirous to mystify the jury, and was told to retire.'

Another witness, Thomas Askey, a clock and spectacle maker of New Buildings, spoke of the pistols saying:

Webb came to my house and wished me to show him a pair of pistols. I did so and he asked for some caps to try them. He purchased the one now produced for 4s. 6d ... about 10 o'clock the next morning Webb came again and purchased the other pistol. I also sold him a bullet mould, he wished me to let him have some bullets, which he saw lying on the counter, but I told him I could not spare them ...

Askey's statement was followed by that of an elderly woman called Clara Barker, who told the inquest that she had seen Webb in the shop, but when he saw her he turned his face away hoping she would not recognize him. She stated she knew Webb well and knowing he and his wife were at variance she suspected he was up to no good. She afterwards asked Askey what Webb had bought and was told a metal toothpick. All the evidence given and the jury brought in a verdict of Wilful Murder on Eliza Webb.

The jury then had to hold an inquest on the death of Webb himself. John Harris a carrier from Barnacle was first to give evidence he said:

I was in the street with my cart, near to the Holly Bush, and heard a report of firearms. Someone [Hopkins] *came up to me and said, 'For God's sake go into the Black Dog, the landlord has shot two persons, but take care of yourself, for he has got two pistols, and he may shoot you.'*

The carrier was made of stronger stuff than Hopkins and Taylor, and continued:

I immediately went and with some difficulty got into the room. It was with considerable effort I was enabled to force open the door and before entering I took off my cap and placing it on my hand, shoved it between the door and door post, thinking that if he saw it he would fire at that instead of me and then I could go in and master him. No firing however took place; and when I went in I found Mrs. Webb lying on her right side, just within the door, quite dead and Webb lying near her.

I lifted up his head and found his face completely blown to pieces, every feature being destroyed. I saw there was no hope for him and laid his head on the floor again; he sighed twice and then expired.

The court commended the carrier for his bravery.

Elizabeth Webb, wife of Nelson Webb's brother and landlady of the *Pilot* in Much Park Street was next to give evidence. She stated that shortly before four o'clock on Saturday afternoon Nelson came to their bar and looked very dark about the eyes. She asked him if he had been taking anything, to which he replied, 'No, it's want of rest makes me look so ill. I have never slept once since last Tuesday night.'

Elizabeth offered him a cup of tea, but Nelson said he just wanted to see his brother, saying, 'If I don't see him soon I'm sure my heart will break!' She said Nelson then went upstairs walking around and whistling seemingly as if he did not know what he was doing.

Perhaps the goriest moment of the day was when the actual bodies of Nelson and Eliza Webb were laid on the floor before the inquest in an upper room of the *Holly Bush*. The bodies were placed as they had been found on the day in question. The *Coventry Herald* reporter says:

The appearance of the bodies … was the most sickening and awful spectacle we ever beheld. There lay a young woman of agreeable countenance still unruffled, and little changed in death. The fatal ball having perforated the side of her head. The man mauled and gory, and all the front of his skull and the upper part of his face absolutely blown away.

St Peter's, Hillfields, where Nelson Webb was given a suicide's burial. Coventry City
Libraries, Local Studies

The jury consulted over three hours on Webb. There were
difficulties in reaching a verdict as one man was said to be,
'very officious and talkative' objecting to the decision saying,
'I don't like the thought of a man being buried in a ditch.' This
probably relates to the fact that often suicides where buried at
road junctions. Eventually he backed down and a verdict of *felo
de se*; self-inflicted suicide was given.

The remains of Nelson Webb were buried by his friends at
St Peter's churchyard in Hillfields. The event excited
considerable interest and thousands attended the burial,
which took place between nine and ten o'clock on the
following Tuesday night. It was reported that Webb's body was
taken in a hearse followed by two mourning coaches. One
person tried to say a few words at the grave but was ordered
to desist, as suicides received no funeral rites by law. Eliza
Webb was buried in the same cemetery the following
afternoon.

CHAPTER 15

The Horrific Murder of Mrs Kington 1859

On 19 November 1859 the *Coventry Standard* reported:

On Saturday morning last [12 Nov.] *a murder, attended by circumstances of peculiar atrocity, was committed within the precincts of this city. The murderer is John Kington, a young man, twenty-two years of age, son of a weaver, respectable in his station of life, residing in South Street. The victim was his own wife* [Elizabeth Ann], *a year or two younger than her husband, daughter of a man named Holmes, formerly in the city police force, from which he was discharged for drunkenness* [this statement later proved false], *and who now resides in a court in Jordan Well.*

It appears that Kington was formerly a drummer in the 1st Warwick Militia and volunteered to join the regiment but was turned down for medical reasons as he suffered from fits. During his time in the militia and elsewhere he was said to have acquired, 'pilfering habits'. Before they were married his wife had had an illegitimate child with a carpenter, who then left her and went to Birmingham. The child soon after died.

Shortly afterwards she met Kington when they were both lodging at a house in Mill Lane [Cox Street]. Rumours began to circulate about their intimacy and Kington later admitted to marrying to halt the rumours. The rumours, at least of the girl's condition, were correct for four months later a child was born. The couple moved into a court in East Street, but the marriage was not a happy one.

It would appear that the couple parted and Kington sold his most valuable possessions and left for London while his wife kept the rest and moved back in with her father. In June 1858 Kington returned and took lodgings in Freeth Street. He talked his wife into returning to him and the couple sold what

Freeth Street where the Kingtons lived was to the right of the motorcar. The entrance to the street has the word 'Leicester' on the wall. Although this photograph was taken around 1929 it remained much as it was in 1859.

remained of their goods. It was reported that between June and August Kington must have lived off the money as he did no work, except when acting as a blackleg for a couple of weeks at Hart's weaving mill off West Orchard, when the workers were out on strike.

Kington's state of mind was not good, and he became jealous and suspicious about his wife and her relationship with her father. In the words of the press:

> *Probably the interference of the wife's father in their quarrels, coupled with the wife's behaviour towards himself, and apparent reliance on her father, gave rise to a suspicion in Kington's morbid jealous and exacting mind, as to the objects to the visits of his wife to her father, a suspicion too horrible to be expressed in print ... His conduct previously bad enough, became* terrible, in fact the *woman was so brutally ill-used, that it was nec. .ary to procure medical advice and Mr. Dresser* [the first surgeon to later see her dead] *attended her.*

One night after being threatened in her bed by Kington with a knife and a razor, she left him, under the protection of a policeman. The next day at the request of her father, a policeman escorted her through the streets so she could apply for a warrant for her husband's apprehension. Kington was brought before the bench and admitted his behaviour trying to excuse it by saying she had spoken ill of his friends, a witness, however, brought to the magistrate's attention the real reason – her alleged unnatural relationship with her father. Kington was bound over and ordered to pay a surety for his peaceful behaviour over the next three months. He failed to pay the surety and was instead imprisoned at Warwick, where it was noted he still suffered from fits.

His wife continued at Mrs Thornett's attended only by her brother, not her father and her child was 'put out at nurse'. Eventually Kington's father paid his bail and he returned to Coventry, staying at his father's house. Kington tried to get his wife to return but she refused as he was not earning and she could not keep, him, herself and their child on the 10 shillings a week she earned at Eli Green's once famous triangular weaving factory.

Still Kington followed her trying to talk her around, but without result. On following her to her father's house he made another appeal, which was refused, and soon a violent quarrel erupted between him, her father and brothers. Kington left to brood all night.

The following morning his wife helped her landlady with some housework before going to work at quarter to seven and calling at her father's, where she had breakfast and walked with her brother for safety to work. The couple reached Harnall Row and there met Kington, who had been waiting for their arrival. Words passed and he pushed the brother aside and demanded his wife go with him, she refused and they struggled. The brother, however, decided at this unfortunate point to leave them to it, as he would be late for work.

The press takes up the story:

Against her will, the woman is, as it were, forced along South Street and the lane at the back of Gosford Street, slowly stopping occasionally ... against the increasing torrent of his fierce wrath ... Fully aware of her danger, she was yet so little impressed by it, that she took no steps to get out of her husbands power ... and when as he forced her into Swan Lane, she was sufficiently roused to do something for her protection, she took the tame step of asking a milk boy to send a policeman after them ... They went along Swan Lane, through the fields leading thence to Payne's Lane, and as soon as they got through the posts which lead into the last of those fields, within sight of Payne's Lane, in a much frequented footpath, and necessarily within hearing of many people ... the fearful deed was performed.

The press then tell the grisly details of the horrific murder stating:

> *Immediately on getting through the posts the ruffian seized the poor creature, who had just endeavoured to run away from him, round the waist, threw her upon the ground, and placing one knee on her chest, the other leg astride over her, proceeded, with the ferocity of an enraged tiger, to cut and mangle her throat and face, in the savage endeavour to sever her head completely from her body. Finding that he could not get the head entirely off, he was tearing out the windpipe, when the cry of a man startled him, and he jumped up quivering with rage, and grinning and grinding his teeth. Other persons were momentarily on the spot. The murderer quietly dropped the knife, he had been using, adjusted the dress of the dead woman and expressed himself ready to go to the Station house.*

Kington was taken back and later, still covered in blood, appeared before two magistrates for examination. The first witness was Sergeant Salmon who said:

> *I received information that a murder had been committed near Payne's Lane, in the first field. I went in search of the prisoner and met him near Day's factory. He said, 'Mr. Salmon, I'm here, I done it, she's dead enough; if you had not come here I should have come to the station.' He walked quietly back with me. I had another constable with me and directed him to go to the body and there remain. When I met the prisoner, he was with a labouring man ... who was going with him for the purpose of giving him into custody ... After taking the man to the station I returned to the body. It was in the first field leading out of Payne's Lane, near the Parsonage house, at the back of Primrose Hill, near the posts.*

Sergeant Salmon then said he acquired a door on which the body was placed and carried to the *Binley Oak* public house and William Dresser the surgeon was sent for to examined the body he would report that the cut to the throat was, 'cleverly done'. Salmon then said that Kington had done it, and meant to and he was under bail, which was not up. To this Kington

The Binley Oak *had this new façade put on in 1895. The surgeon brought the body of Mrs Kington here to examine it and the inquest was held here while her body remained in an outbuilding.* John Ashby/David McGrory Collection

replied, 'The time is up today. She should not have been ruled by her father, she should have been ruled by me. Her father was the whole cause of it.' Salmon added that the prisoner had told him that her last words were, 'Jack, Jack, its my father's fault.' Kington butted in saying, she said, 'It's my father's fault, God bless you, good bye.' The latter part of this statement seems improbable under the circumstances.

The inquest was held in the presence of the corpse, which was displayed in an outbuilding at the *Binley Oak*, the first witness being Henry Quinney a fourteen-year-old milk boy from Stoke, who said that he had come across the couple in Swan Lane. Quinney heard Kington say, 'I only asked you how yourself was, and the child,' she replied, 'It's nothing to do with you,' he responded, 'It's all to do with me.' Quinney noticed Kington forcing his wife up the lane against her will and she called to him to fetch a policeman, but he did not.

Another witness who knew both was Mary Ann Pickard who stated that she was on her way to work at Jeffrey Wood's Cross, when she heard screams and looked over a hedge, she saw Kington throw his wife to the ground and brandish a knife. She says, 'She put her hands together and asked him to forgive her twice. He said, no he'd forgiven her times enough; she might thank her father for it all, and if he had been there he'd had served him the same. Whilst he was making use of those words he was cutting her throat.'

The graphic description continued
in the girl's words:

*He put his hand to her throat and
said, 'I'll pull it out' I went into the
field and saw her give two kicks, he
then stabbed her again. I said, 'You've
done enough now let her be.' When
Kington got up from the woman he
said, 'I can die happy now.' As this
happened James Jones, builder
approached, called Kington a villain,
to which Kington jumped up in a
frenzy, then seeing others approach
calmed down and dropped his knife
saying, according to Jones 'I have*

Kington attacking his wife.

*done what I intended to do, and now I shall die happy. I have not
been allowed to see my child, and not often to see my wife. I have
had my house sold up and been put in prison.'*

James Edmunds, a labourer from Adelaide Street, also
appeared on the scene after being told of the murder. He went
to Kington, who said, 'I've done it; I'd have cut her head off if
I could, but I couldn't, the knife bent.' William Dresser the
surgeon said:

*I was sent for to see the deceased ... I found the body at the Binley
Oak, quite dead. On the right hand side of the head there was a
gash down the cheek, severing the principal arteries of the face.
There was another cut, which was superficial, a little below it; and
the main injury was the throat. The carotid artery was divided,
and in fact all the arteries to the spine, and the windpipe was
severed ... the right hand was also badly cut. It is evident that she
resisted considerably. It was possible for her to have spoken after
the first cut.*

Kington then asked for James Jones again, it had been said
earlier that Jones could have saved the woman if he arrived on
the scene quicker; Kington however claimed he was at the

scene and intended the court to know. Kington claimed Jones was within sight of him before the event saying, 'We walked on before you, and you got within about 40 yards of us.' Jones denied it, saying, 'Oh, dear, dear, I never saw you at all.' Kington said, 'Did you stand where that first tree is cut down and watch me?' 'No,' came the answer. 'You did,' said Kington. 'Never,' said the witness, 'I was more than 300 yards away when I first heard her scream.' Kington then said, 'Didn't that little girl, who went by call you before I touched her?' Jones again denied it and Kington said, 'The little girl called you and you stood against the butt of the tree.' He continued saying, 'And when you saw me taking the knife out didn't she say, Jones, Jones, save me.' Jones denied it and the mayor, interrupted adding that Kington must be mistaken. To this Kington coolly turned his head and said, 'Nobody laughs at me – when she asked you to save her, what did you say – you would have nothing to do with it. You ran across the fields into Payne's Lane, and when you came back you saw me on her, and when you came back I murdered her then.' This caused a sensation in the court, Jones emphatically denied it and the mayor said, 'I fear prisoner these questions won't assist you at all.' 'I don't want them to,' said Kington eagerly, 'I want to die.' This caused more sensation through the court and the mayor asked if he had any other questions for the witness to which Kington replied scathingly, 'I have not, I won't speak to a man as tells lies.'

Some of the previous witnesses were recalled and also a new one, Henry Roe, who seemed to back up Kington's accusation against Jones saying that when he was going into Payne's Lane from Gilbert Street, 'I heard Jones calling to me.' He said, 'For God's sake run, there's a man murdered a woman.' Roe did not run away but claimed to have run to the place of the murder where Kington was cutting his wife's throat. He claimed Kington stood up and raised the knife towards him, to which Kington responded, 'I never seen you, I don't know as I ever seen you before in my life.'

Mr Smallbone who spoke on behalf of the deceased's father gave an unqualified denial to the, 'dreadful accusations which rumour has laid to his charge, which he stigmatised as most foul and calumnious. He was prepared to prove that there was not the slightest ground for the rumour.' The coroner, however, said that he could not hear the evidence, as it was not revelant.

Finally the coroner summed up the case and commended the girl Pickard for her bravery, but not before he had warned Quinney to take more note of what people told him. The coroner Alfred Carter concluded by saying:

> *It might occur to them that some provocation had been given but it was his duty to tell them that no provocation in mere words could justify one human being killing another. This, however, appeared to be an unprovoked and premeditated murder. There had been a rumour that something wrong had taken place between the deceased and her father, but that seemed to be mere idle rumour, and must be treated as such. It was well ascertained that if a man caught his wife in the act of adultery, and in the first transport of passion killed her, it would be manslaughter and not murder. But if it were merely from a suspicion, however strong, that she was carrying on an illicit intrigue, such a killing would be murder.*

The case was sent for trial.

Before the trial the press contained reports on Kington's criminal record; he was said when in the militia to be quick tempered and would make a rush for his bayonet whatever the offence. In 1854 he was sentenced to fourteen days hard labour for stealing a handkerchief and in October that year went to gaol for six months for stealing a waistcoat. In 1857 he was convicted for assaulting a woman, and failing to pay the fine went to gaol for fourteen days. Then there was his imprisonment after assaulting his wife. During his time in Coventry Gaol while awaiting trial he received visits from his mother, father, brother and sisters and during this time it is said that Kington realized his fate suffering the horrors of the gallows, having sleepless nights and sometimes bursting into tears. He did, however, then and throughout his last days, believe that he, not his wife was the victim. At the beginning of December he was transferred to Warwick Gaol. The transfer was supposed to be secret but huge crowds followed him to Coventry station. On the train it was reported that Kington was, very depressed and tears rolled down his cheeks.

On Tuesday, 21 December 1859 Kington faced trial at Warwick County Hall under the direction of Mr Justice Williams. John Kington in an almost inaudible voice pleaded guilty. The judge said, 'I trust prisoner that you have not taken this course under any persuasion that it will in any degree lighten the sentence that may be passed upon you.' Kington replied, 'No, Sir (taking a paper from his pocket and handing it to the court). I wish this to be read in court, sir.' The judge read the paper and said, 'I suppose you do not wish it to be read publicly?' Kington replied, 'Yes sir, I wish it to be read openly.'

Kington called for the Reverend Mr Widdrington of St Michael's to read it, who had visited him a number of times in gaol and had encouraged him to plead guilty. The reverend gentleman was brought forward and said the prisoner had made a mistake, for he had advised him to let the judge alone see the document, saying, 'I thought the circumstances which are represented in that paper might, if it were possible, weigh with you, and that the extreme penalty of the law might be substituted by a sentence of less awful character.'

Judge Williams then said if the prisoner wished it read he could not prevent it, after which the Reverend Mr Widdrington said to Kington, 'You had better not have it read.' To which Kington replied, 'I wish to have it read in public.' The reverend pulled him close and a discussion took place.' As they parted the judge said, 'What now, have it read?', to which Kington replied, 'No.'

Kington was then asked if he had anything to say before sentence was pronounced, he made no answer and silence was called in court. Justice Williams placed the black cap upon his head and with a trembling voice, he said:

Prisoner at the bar, you have been found guilty upon your own confession of the murder of your wife. I have read through the depositions of the witnesses before the coroner and the committing magistrates … and finding their evidence conclusive … to deny guilt would have only led to useless pain ... You hand in a paper which I have read ... but am bound to say that nothing I have read in that paper would justify me in holding out to you the slightest hope that mercy will be extended to you in this case. I have begged you not to insist upon having the paper read in public. I do so because it contains imputations upon others of the most dreadful kind, which I believe to be unfounded – which you believe to be unfounded – and should indeed regret that your last act in this world should have been one of such dreadful horror as to impute to any living being the crimes which are mentioned in that paper ... The sentence of the court upon you is, that you be taken from hence to the place whence you came, thence to the place of execution, that you be hanged by your neck till you are dead, and that you shall be buried within the precincts of the gaol, and may God have mercy on your soul.

It is said that, through his time awaiting execution in Warwick Gaol, Kington was generally calm and collected, spending much time with the Bible and in prayers. His opinion changed on many things except for his sure belief that he was the victim. His family visited him and took his infant son to see him for the last time; most of what happened at the meeting is not recorded. But as they were leaving the chief turnkey remembering Kington had often said his wife said the child did not belong to him, mentioned the strong likeness the child seemed to have to Kington. Kington seemed affected by this but stayed silent. At his request the blood splattered clothes he wore during the murder were sent to him as he intended to wear them during his execution.

The following day, Friday, 30 December being the day of the execution, he rose at seven o'clock, and began reading. He then went to a service in the chapel and at one point looked slightly affected. He also wrote two letters to his parents asking them to bring the child up, 'like one of your own' and to give his sisters and brothers his prayer books and Bible. He said he was prepared for death thanks to the chaplains of both Coventry and Warwick and repented his sins and believed he would be saved and 'rewarded' in heaven. He concluded by saying, 'I now conclude dear Father and Mother, brothers and

sisters, and all friends, wishing you all goodbye and God bless
you, and I hope and trust we may meet again in heaven.
Farewell. John Kington.'

The press report continued:

*Thence he went to the pinioning room, where his arms were
pinioned. He wore the same dress as at the trial, and of course not
that in which he committed the murder … He frequently sighed
but was otherwise calm. In the chain room the chaplain prayed
and bade a last farewell … Accompanied by the Under Sheriff,
Mr. Adkins, the gaoler, Mr. Machouocie, the chief turnkey, three
officers and the hangman (Smith of Dudley who executed
Palmer) the murderer proceeded to the gallows, which is situated
on a platform over the door of the prison, in Bridewell Lane.
From an early hour in the morning people had been flocking to
the spot to witness the terrible scene, and an immense multitude
now thronged the lane, and the open space beyond it, where
several streets join.*

*The assemblage was not so large as it would have been if the
hour of the execution had
been made known. The
train leaving Coventry at
fifteen minutes past ten
was literally crammed
with people anxious to be
spectators, but who were
too late. It was twenty
minutes past ten o'clock
as the doomed man
stepped on the scaffold. He
requested to be allowed to
address the multitude and
was informed that his
wish would be complied
with. The rope was then
adjusted round his neck,
after which he advanced
to the railings, which
border the platform and*

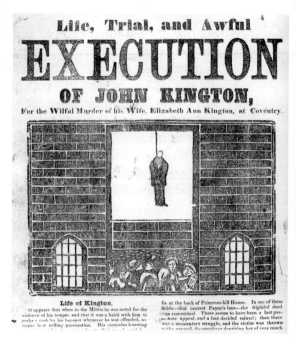

An execution broadside as would have been sold to
one of the spectators at the hanging of John Kington.
Coventry City Libraries, Local Studies

said, 'My dear friends,' but his voice choked and he could not proceed. Somewhat agitated he remarked to those near him, 'Oh, I cannot speak.' After a short pause he said, 'I will try again,' and raising his voice, tremulously pronounced, 'My dear friends, I hope you will take warning' – but he could speak no further and stepped back, saying he would pray.

He was then readied for execution and agreed to drop a handkerchief to signal the hangman. The black hood was placed over his head and he repeated the 'General Confession' and the Lord's Prayer with a great fervour. Then, as the press reported:

He had scarcely concluded, when he let fall the handkerchief and almost before it touched the ground, the drop fell; a strong convulsive motion of the limbs was perceptible for about two minutes, and then the majesty of the law was vindicated – the murderer swung lifeless in the air. After hanging for an hour and five minutes the body was cut down, and a cast of the head was taken by Mr. E. T. Craig, a phrenologist, who had obtained the requisite permission. ... The body was buried in the Gaol on Friday afternoon.

One fact few mentioned was that as Kington had a thick neck, the drop failed and did not produce instantaneous death by dislocation. Kington was in fact slowly strangled, a slow death, which took nearly two minutes.

The victim, Elizabeth Ann Kington, was taken in a black hearse from her father's house in Gosford Street, followed by her father and brothers in a black mourning coach. The funeral cortege was followed by a crowd numbering up to 3,000 people, to St Peter's Church in Hillfields. It was reported in the press that the incumbent performed an 'impressive' service and noted that, 'though much popular indignation had been aroused towards the father of the deceased, there was, we are glad to be able to state, but little expression of it.'

CHAPTER 16

The Fawson Murder and Suicide 1860

In February 1860 the inhabitants of Coventry were just recovering from the Kington murder when it happened again. A butcher, Henry Fawson, the son of John Fawson formerly of the *Three Crowns* in Gosford Street had some years earlier married Charlotte, daughter of Charles Sumner, a maltster and publican who lived in Butcher Row. The marriage was a very happy one by all accounts, but within four or five months Henry Fawson for some reason suspected his wife of infidelity. The couple split up and Fawson left the shop he had been trading from in Spon Street. Charlotte Fawson's father, however, compelled Fawson to maintain his daughter; this Fawson did and after a short time became the tenant of a small house in a yard off Smithford Street.

From there some sort of reconciliation took place and Charlotte moved back in with her husband. All appeared well, until one morning Fawson left saying he was going to the fair, but instead he caught a train to Nuneaton, then Liverpool, from where he took passage to America. Sometime during his absence Charlotte had a child, who died. Fawson returned to Coventry three years later and resumed his trade of butcher based in Junction Street, Hillfields. Promises were made to maintain Charlotte but no money was forthcoming.

Smithford Street where the Fawsons lived before the murder photographed around 1860.

Again Charlotte became pregnant and again the child died, whether this was Fawson's child is not known, but again she moved back to her husband, and those who knew them said they appeared to be happy. Fawson kept himself busy in the shop and very occasionally Charlotte would be seen to help if the day was particularly busy.

The press said at the time, 'Both were persons of agreeable appearance, and Fawson was a man of a jocose and lively turn.' It appears on the night on which the tragedy occurred, he went to visit relations, and seeming more sedate than usual told them that business was good and that he intended to buy a bigger house. The press continued the story:

A little after nine he returned home and served a customer with a mutton chop. This was the last occasion on which either husband or wife were seen alive. Mrs. Fawson was then sitting by the kitchen fire. Nothing more is heard of them till a little before two o'clock, when the neighbours on each side, separated from Fawson's room by a single brick wall only, are aroused from their sleep by faint cries of 'Murder' in a female voice.

Both neighbours got out of bed and listened. One cried out, 'What is the matter', a deep groan was the only response and silence again prevails. As the listeners settled themselves again to rest, they little thought that, separated from them by so narrow a partition, lay a woman with her throat cut and in the agonies of death, and that her murderer, with his wind-pipe cut through, was groping down stairs for his gun, with which to blow out his own brains. A heavy fall three quarters of an hour after this first alarm marked the time at which the dreadful tragedy concluded, and the murderer was hurried, by his own act, into another world.

The neighbours did not, however, respond assuming the sounds were coming from someone in great pain from illness. There were no further developments until the following morning. At 9.30 am, unusually, the butcher's shop was still closed and repeated knocking on the door produced no response. It was decided to force an entry so a ladder was obtained, and a back bedroom window broken. The press continues:

A policeman and two other persons entered the chamber and passed into the front apartment, where [Fawson was found] lying on the ground with nothing on but his shirt, surrounded by a sickening mass of brains and blood, with which the walls and ceiling were also disfigured.

Finding that the wound in his neck did not produce speedy death; he had inserted the muzzle of a gun into his mouth, and so discharged its contents into his head. The female was lying upon the bed with her throat cut in such a manner as to produce speedy death. The skill of the butcher had been brought to bear in her murder. Instead of adopting the common notion of cutting from ear to ear, the miserable man had cut the lower part of her neck, thereby ensuring the opening of the carotid artery, but it appears that the windpipe was not injured, which accounts for the poor woman's cries after her death wound was inflicted.

This was done while she was asleep, there is little doubt, as her hands are not only free from cuts, but are not even marked with blood, as they must have been had she used them to defend herself. The gun was discovered lying in the fender of the bedroom, while the fatal knife was found covered with blood, on the table downstairs, where it had been placed when Fawson went to fetch the gun. It may appear extraordinary, that though he did, undoubtedly go down stairs for this purpose, no trace of blood was found on the stairs or in the lower room. It seems however, that no important arteries were injured, so that the discharge of blood would not be great and what did flow was absorbed by his shirt.

The inquest was held at the *Elephant and Castle* in Hillfields where a jury of fourteen were sworn in and viewed the bodies. A verdict of wilful murder was given on Charlotte Fawson. The inquest was then held on the body of Henry Fawson and witnesses were heard including Dr Goate who attended the incident. He said apart from the small 'incised wound' to the upper throat Fawson had two shallow stab wounds, one on his right and one on his left hand side and he concluded that he had failed to kill himself with a clasp knife and instead used his own double barrel shot gun.

George Furnival who had been employed by Fawson for seven months stated that when he last saw him, 'he was as

The Elephant and Castle, *Hillfields where the inquest on the Fawsons was held.*

lively as he was generally'. Interestingly Furnival knew of the gun, stating that it had been kept loaded over the previous fortnight and since then one barrel had been fired. He also stated to the jury that he did not recognize the clasp knife used in the murder and that Fawson usually carried a small pocket knife.

Fawson's sister testified that she had seen him that night and although he seemed a little quiet and not so jocular as usual he appeared quite well. As there appeared to be no obvious reason for the event, a juror asked if Fawson had suffered from insanity. The coroner concluded that the deceased was sane when he murdered his wife, and indeed, it was said, there was no evidence, 'not the slightest shadow of proof of any insanity'. He summed up by saying he 'supposed' that the only conclusion could be that Fawson had murdered himself after having murdered his wife.

The jury retired and after two hours, twelve out of fourteen agreed to a verdict of *felo de se*, death by suicide. Henry Fawson was buried without rites in the churchyard of St Peter's in Hillfields at eleven o'clock at night, amongst a vast throng of people. Charlotte's body was returned to her brother who lived at the *Spotted Dog* in the Bull Ring to await burial.

Amongst the people of Coventry there was much speculation about this case as there seemed to be too many unanswered questions. The Fawsons appeared to all to be happy, and witnesses said they had never heard a cross word pass between them. Also Fawson had two stab wounds in his sides, and many considered it odd that a butcher, skilled with the knife and in despatching animals, should fail in cutting his own throat and strangely stab himself in his sides before going downstairs, but leaving no bloodstains, not even a bloody hand-print. Yet he had apparently just cut his wife's throat with the unidentified clasp knife he was carrying and which was covered in blood. It would, in any case, have seemed more logical that he would have used a butcher's knife from the shop. Furthermore, after spending nearly three quarters of an hour in the kitchen and putting the knife on the table, no blood, not so much as a smudge, was to be found. He then took his already loaded gun back upstairs before finally shooting himself. Other unexplained factors were the questionable children that Charlotte had given birth to, Henry's strange disappearance to America, and the reasons behind his recently felt need to keep a loaded shotgun in the house. All questions that will remain forever unanswered.

CHAPTER 17

The Hillfield's Poisoner
1861

The *Coventry Herald and Observer* reported on Friday, 23 August 1861 that an inquest had been held on the suspicious death, on 20 August, of one Betsy Beamish, the wife of a respectable, but indiscreet ex-Sunday school teacher and weaver, William Beamish of Spencer Street, Hillfields. The first witness at the inquest held at the *Gloucester Arms* on the Stoney Stanton Road was Dr Goate who stated that the deceased's husband had called him to their home on 16 August and he found Betsy, 'very ill, complaining of a pain in the chest and throat … she had taken breakfast an hour before and thrown it all up again'.

Betsy Beamish informed the doctor that she had suffered the same trouble over the previous several days. The doctor gave her medicine and visited her each day until Sunday, after which on Monday and Tuesday she sent him word, that she was getting better all the time. Then on Tuesday morning William Beamish called at the doctor's house to inform him that his wife was dead, and asked him to write a death certificate, the doctor refused telling Beamish that the case

Houses in Spencer Street. Coventry City Libraries, Local Studies

needed looking into. At this point Dr Goate said Beamish looked agitated. He did, however, later issue a certificate stating that Betsy had died of 'castrius'.

On the Wednesday Goate and William Dresser the surgeon performed an autopsy and found nothing to explain the woman's death, except a slight inflammation of the stomach. Both men, however, concluded that Betsy Beamish appeared to have died from poisoning and they placed samples from the stomach, liver and transverse colon into a jar and sent it to be examined by a chemical expert, Dr Wrightson of Birmingham.

The second witness Jane Stokes told the inquest that on the Wednesday she had visited the house and Betsy was vomiting, as were her three children. The two eldest recovered but the next day the youngest died. She said that Betsy told her that all of them had been taken ill following their breakfast. The third witness Emma Statham of Albert Street, of whom we will hear more later, said that she was employed at the house of the deceased and said that she was with Betsy when she died. The inquest was then adjourned until Dr Wrightson's analysis was available.

In the next edition of the *Herald and Observer* on the 30 August, we are informed, 'Wm. Beamish, weaver, Jane Stokes, wife of Mark Stokes, and Emma Statham, were brought into custody, charged with administering poison to Betsy Beamish, wife of the male prisoner'. It appears that Inspector Payne, acting on the belief of Dr Goate and Mr Dresser arrested Beamish, who coincidentally at the time of his arrest had a packet in his breast pocket labelled, 'Watson, Broadgate', 'Poison'. Upon searching his house the inspector's men also found in the pocket of a pair of trousers, another empty paper bearing the words, 'Poison – Jenkin's Chemist, Smithford Street'. Payne cautioned Beamish and asked him what had become of the contents of this packet to which Beamish replied he had mixed it with oats to kill the rats and mice in his garden. Jane Stokes and Emma Statham were also arrested as both of them had spent time with Betsy Beamish before her final demise.

The following morning the garden was searched for remains of the poisoned oats, but nothing was found. On that same day Payne received a letter from Jane Stokes claiming she had seen Beamish take the paper from the pocket of one of his wife's

The Gloucester Arms *where the inquest took place.* John Ashby/David McGGrory Collection

dresses. Stokes and Statham were released but Beamish remained in custody until after the inquest.

On the 26 August the inquest resumed, 'on Betsy Beamish who died in Spencer Street on Tuesday, the 20th instant, under suspicious circumstances'. It is said on that day that the *Gloucester Arms* was packed to 'suffocation' and outside stood a crowd numbering up to seven hundred people.

The first witness was Charlotte Wright who lived next door at 29 Spencer Street. She testified that her daughter had told her on the day in question that Betsy and her children were ill, so she went to visit and found Betsy vomiting in the kitchen. When asked if she'd eaten anything that disagreed with her Betsy replied, 'Oh, no, we have only had some coffee, and the children have had some bread and dripping and some bread and treacle, and to tell the truth, I was eating a bit of dry bread myself.' Charlotte Wright saw her again some hours later in the yard and said, 'You look ill', to which she replied, 'I feel very ill indeed'. She did not see her again until Friday morning when Jane Stokes asked her if she wished to see her and Jane Stokes asked her to give Betsy her medicine, which she immediately brought up again.

Charlotte Wright said, 'I did not see the baby, she said the baby had been very sick' and when further questioned about the couple's relationship said they seemed comfortable and did not argue much. She then added more, which hinted to another part of Beamish's character, 'I have heard of Beamish's gay goings on, but I have never seen him with any females, nor do I know of my own knowledge that he has been with any.' She concluded by saying of the child that died shortly before, 'The first time I had known her to be sick was on the 14th instant ... The child had not been ill long. The day before the death it seemed quite well ... was playing up and down the yard. I did not see her again until she was dead; she died on the Tuesday.'

The next witness was Emily Harrow, Betsy Beamish's sister, she said:

> *I went with her to the cemetery to bury the little child. When we came back from the cemetery she asked me to take her to the closet, and when there she put her arms around me and said, 'Millie, was your mouth like mine when you got better of the cholera,' and I said, 'Let me see,' ... the tongue was very red and very dry ...*

Betsy Beamish also told her sister that it was painful to pass water. She then left the closet and with the assistance of William, who was always attentive, she was put to bed. Her sister gave her tea, which was kept warm in the oven and she asked for arrowroot, which Emma Statham took from the oven. She was given this by her sister and was immediately sick.

Dr Wrightson, an analytical chemist who had actually tested the results of taking poisons on himself, then appeared and informed the court that after a number of tests he found the stomach contained enough arsenic to cause death and concluded that, 'I am of the opinion that death ensued from poisoning by arsenic'.

John Bennett was then sworn in, and said:

> *I am an apprentice to Mr. Jenkins, chemist and druggist, Smithford Street, and I serve in his shop. On the 17th of August a man who called himself William Beamish came to our shop about eleven o'clock in the day and asked for three pennyworth of arsenic. I said I could not let him have it without he brought a witness with him. He then went out and returned about ten o'clock at night, accompanied by another man as a witness. I then let him have the arsenic and wrote his name in a book, and the*

witness put his name in the book also. The arsenic was coloured a
bluish colour, but I cannot say with what. Mr. Jenkins cautioned
him as to the dangerous nature of the article he was purchasing,
and he merely said it was for the rats.

Later Joseph Pollard who worked at the chemist shop of
Richard Watson in Broadgate was called. He testified that
Beamish had been in his employer's shop on 17 August and
asked for arsenic, which they did not stock. A concoction
called, 'crow-fig' was recommended and Beamish returned on
another occasion, asked what it tasted like and purchased a
pennyworth. Pollard advised him to add it to oatmeal and he
would soon, 'find something dead'. The packet that had
contained it was found in Beamish's breast pocket at the time
of his arrest, and it was then shown to the court.

The next witness, J. Parkes of 18 Victoria Street who was a
chemist, then appeared, and he told the inquest that Beamish
had also been to him in search of arsenic. Parkes had said he
did not stock it to which Beamish replied that he had sold
some to him previously mixed with soft soap. Parkes recalled
that he had actually sold Beamish the arsenic for vermin two
months previously.

Jane Stokes was then recalled and asked about a claimed
suicide note, which was read out:

For Jane Stokes, Dr. Sister – if anything happens to me doo not
let them blame anyone but me for god forgive me I did not know
what I was doing but the thought of loseing my home and to see
how the poor lad was fretin to know wat to do for the moment
drove me mad for to lose my home I could not bare the disgrace
after living respectful so long and do not tel him if you can elp it
for it will drive him mad Jane see to the little on for he is so fond
of Lizzey God bles and comfort my poor lad.
Betsy Beamish 14th Aug.

Jane Stokes told the inquest that after his wife's death Beamish
had suggested that they check Betsy's dresses which they did
and in the dress she wore on the day she was first taken ill
Beamish found the note and after glancing at it appeared to be

thrown in an agitated state. She afterwards gave the letter to Inspector Payne. The note seemed to reflect Betsy's worries about money and the thought of losing her home. However, there was one major problem concerning this suicide note: Jane Stokes said, 'I have never seen or known her to write. As far as I know she had not been to school, but she could read. William Beamish can write; I have seen him write plenty of times ...'

When asked if she had witnessed Beamish act improperly she denied it, then on being pressed said that she remembered when a girl called Callaghan came to see Emma Statham and as Beamish sat by the fire with them she believed his behaviour, improper considering that his wife lay ill upstairs.

Inspector Payne then testified before the inquest was adjourned, the jury, 'retiring to examine the body of the child that had been exhumed'. As Beamish left the inquest it was reported that the crowds, 'hissed and groaned in a fearful manner'. During the adjournment stories began to circulate in the city regarding Beamish's relationship with Emma Statham, and both were greeted with a deafening storm of yells and hisses whenever seen in public.

The inquest resumed on the following Monday and eyes then turned to the alleged suicide note and the need to compare it with Beamish's hand. The Reverend Phillip Baker of Well Street Chapel gave evidence, stating that up until eighteen months ago Beamish was a teacher in the Sunday school. He was handed a letter addressed by Beamish but told the inquest he was unable to recognize the hand, and also had no knowledge of whether or not Betsy Beamish could write.

Mr Powell, a schoolmaster for forty years, then appeared. He informed the inquest that he had a letter from Beamish and believed that it and the suicide note were different hands. The suicide note he believed was in the hand of a woman or child.

The next witness, Sarah Turner, lived at 17 Spencer Street opposite the Beamishs and had known the couple for about eight years. She turned the inquest on its head when asked about Beamish's private life, saying:

He has always been very kind and affectionate to her till within the last eighteen months – ever since he became acquainted with

Emma Statham. I first saw Emma Statham with Beamish alone together about 14 months ago. They were sitting on the grass amongst the trees near the Stivichall Arms. It was getting dusk. They were sitting a short distance from the road ... His arm was round her waist, and her hand in his ... William Beamish could not help but see me. The next time I saw them was at a public house – the Shepherd and Shepherdess on the Keresley Road. It was in the afternoon. They were in the parlour. There was no one with them ... I had an errand in the neighbourhood, and called at the public house for a glass of ale. I sat down in the bar to drink it, and while there saw them together. Beamish was kissing her and their hands were together. I saw through the door ... I did not go into the room where they were ... The next time I saw them was coming out of Nutt's liquor shop in Cross Cheaping ... and he could not help but see me ... The next time I saw them was in Tew's Lane [Swan Lane]. It was between ten and eleven o'clock at night ... His arm was round her waist, and he was kissing her. As I passed by them she said, 'I think there is somebody coming.' He replied that he did not mind who was coming; he was sworn to have her and do all he could for her. That conversation took place while I was passing by.

She then concluded by saying that she had often seen them together in his loom shop, through the large window. They were often alone and they were always kissing and messing about. 'I saw them in the shop together ... last Friday,' she

The Shepherd and Shepherdess *at Keresley Heath where Beamish was seen with Emma Statham in the parlour.*

said, 'I saw him put his hand up her petticoat and kiss her.' All this was observed from her bedroom and attic, which gave good views into Beamish's loom shop. She had once told Betsy about seeing the couple and she said that she could never go out without being told of his goings on.

Another neighbour had a disposition read out stating that, 'I thought it my duty to watch him when he was carrying on like that'. More damning evidence came via Elizabeth Cox, landlady of the *Rose* in West Orchard, she stated that Beamish and Statham had been into her bar several times over the last year and often ate supper there, stating that, 'I always thought from their manner and conduct that they were parties courting.'

Dr Wrightson then appeared and informed the inquest that he had completed his tests and had found arsenic in all the organs supplied to him and said he believed it had been taken in several doses. He also stated that Dr Goate had given him similar samples taken from the body of the Beamish child and in those he had also discovered arsenic. The child, he said, died quickly after the poison entered his body.

Next to give evidence was Jane Stokes to whom the coroner immediately apologized, saying he was annoyed that she had been taken into custody when there was no evidence to implicate her in the crime. She told the court that she was with Betsy the night before she died and had reprimanded her for saying she was going, however Betsy had said, 'If I don't see you again, remember I am happy.' She added that she had been holding the child when it died and Betsy only complained about her husband staying out late and did not mention anything concerning Statham. She also pointed out that strangely, Beamish had not attended the funeral of his child.

Statham was then called and approached the stand laughing and giggling and the coroner had to reprimand her before she finally told the inquest she first began working at Beamish's shop after the weavers' strike in 1860. She denied being with him at Stivichall, and claimed she had been with him and his wife on the Kenilworth Road. She had been with Beamish at the *Shepherd and Shepherdess* but claimed it was in the daytime and being with a couple she came across him on the road and he joined them. She added 'we returned before dark'. She also denied going to Nutt's liquor vaults and said the only time Beamish accompanied her in the direction of Tew Lane was when she worked late and Mrs Beamish told him to. She admitted going to the *Rose* on her own and having 'seen' Beamish there. She said, 'He has never put his arm round my waist – I swear that … He has never put his arms round my waist when I have been in the loom shop with him.'

At this point the coroner pointed out that he was inclined because of her improper and pert manner, her giggling and tossing of hair when answering questions not to believe her evidence regarding her relationship with her employer. The examination continued regarding who prepared food as many assumed the poison had been administered this way. Statham admitted to making gruel and arrowroot for Betsy Beamish on a number of occasions, adding that Mrs Stokes was always there when she did it and as for the tea she claimed Mrs Beamish always made it.

St Mary's Hall, Bayley Lane photographed around the time of the inquest.

The coroner then adjourned the inquest as he wanted a handwriting expert to study the alleged suicide note and it was asked because of the noise from the huge crowd in and around the building that the inquest be moved to somewhere quieter and St Mary's Hall in Bayley Lane was appropriated.

On Saturday, 7 September the inquest restarted in St Mary's Hall. Public interest had grown even more and the *Coventry Herald and Observer* reported that:

> *a crowd of several thousands was collected around the entrance to St. Mary's Hall and it required the efforts of a number of policemen to keep the people from bursting in the door, and overwhelming everyone ... although a sufficient number had been admitted to fill a great part of the body of the hall, the minstrel gallery and every inch of space ...*

It was reported that shortly before the inquest Beamish was walking up and down the yard of the lock up whistling and looking very unconcerned, an attitude he had held throughout the various stages of the inquest. The first witness was John Weston, a registrar who presided at the Beamishs' wedding: he informed the court that he witnessed that Betsy Beamish actually signed her own name in the registry book. This was followed by Thomas Jones the landlord of the *General Wolfe* on the Foleshill Road. He testified that Beamish had often visited his pub in company with a girl called 'Emma'. They would stay about an hour leaving just before the pub closed at ten.

Jones's wife's statement was read out, 'Beamish seemed most attentive to the girl he called, "Emma". I thought he was courting her. I never saw him put his arm around her waist or kiss her. The next witness caused a stir in the hall as William Henry Beamish, the accused's 10-year-old son took the stand and said:

Inside the Great Hall where the inquest took place. Even the minstrel's gallery was packed with spectators.

I remember that morning when we were taken ill. There was myself, my mother and my two sisters; we were at breakfast. We had bread and treacle and a sup of coffee. I had had some coffee when I was taken sick, and some bread and treacle ... My mother had dried bread ... The little baby was taken sick first, my mother next, then me and then Lizzy ... We had some tea, bread and butter for our dinner that day, we were sick after that ... After tea I got pretty well so did Lizzy ... We had never been sick all together before that morning.

William was then shown a small memorandum book, which it had been established, was the source of the paper for the alleged suicide note. He instantly recognized it as belonging to his father and told the jury on the day his baby sister died his father asked him to bring him the notebook and he saw him writing in it. He told the court he had never seen his mother write in the book or Emma Statham. Inspector Payne then took the stand and confirmed the earlier claim from witness Sarah Turner that it was possible to clearly see events happening in the Beamish house from her house.

Next Emma Harper, Beamish's sister took the stand and told the court she lived in Hart's Yard and her brother took a job at James Hart's weaving factory in West Orchard because of the problems in the trade and the threat of poverty. She pointed out that her brother, since he had been at the factory, was in the habit of bringing and having his breakfast with her: bread and butter and coffee, he liked coffee.

Next came John Prestige who said he lived by the side of Harnall Lane in the gardens. He testified that Beamish used one of the gardens and after his wife's death he had gone into the garden looking for peas which Beamish claimed were damaged by vermin, Prestige did not see any damaged peas or traces of the arsenic. He also told the jury he recently talked to Beamish while he was there and he made no mention of vermin, neither had any of the others who rented the gardens.

This was followed by the coroner's London expert who had been given the suicide note and other documents bearing Beamish's handwriting. He took the stand within a hive of murmuring. He said:

My name is Joseph Netherclift ... I am a facsimilist and have been lithographer at the British Museum for 40 years. For the last 30 years I have been employed in giving evidence in Courts of Law as to matters of handwriting. I have carefully examined the handwriting of the papers ... I don't believe the handwriting of the note signed August 14th [suicide note] *is a feigned handwriting ... I should say it was written by a man, but a very ignorant one* [this caused a sensation in the hall]. *You gave me seven notes of paper and I find they are all written by one person.*

He then described to the jury how he had arrived at his conclusion, and ended by saying, 'I would be very sorry to hang a man on such an opinion, but still I have no moral doubt as to its correctness.'

The coroner then summed up and asked the jury to consider all the evidence as to whether Besty Beamish had killed herself and her baby or had been murderered. He told the jury that she had not written the letter and although many chemists can be found who had sold poison to her husband, none can be found that sold it to her. He also pointed out the fact that her husband insisted on searching her dresses and conveniently found the suicide note. There was also, of course, the intimacy with Statham.

The jury retired for twenty-five minutes then returned, the foreman stood up and declared, 'The jury finds that the deceased Betsy Beamish, and her infant daughter, Emily Beamish died from the effects of arsenic, purchased and administered by William Beamish.' He also added that Emma Statham was an accessory before the fact. The coroner, however, interrupted at this point and told the jury he could not accept the final verdict concerning Stratham as there was no evidence showing her complicity in the crime, but he would hear what they had to say. The jury and coroner then retired for a short time into the old council chamber and then retook their places to read out the final verdict: William Beamish guilty of the wilful murder of Besty Beamish and guilty of the wilful murder of Emily Beamish. The inquest was then closed.

On the following Monday Beamish was brought before judges in the County Hall, which was surrounded by a crowd of people.

It is said certain ladies of quality were allowed through the side doors to see the event. Eight hours later after a replay in the hall Beamish was committed to trial for murder at Warwick.

Beamish pleaded not guilty of the charges against him and it was noted at the time that those who dealt with him believed he had intimate knowledge of the notorious Palmer the Poisoner, and also knew minute details concerning his trial and believed the man to be some kind of hero. When asked about Statham, Beamish always said she was innocent and would say no more. Interestingly it came out that shortly before his child died, a boy who worked for Beamish and, 'turned the wheel in his factory' died suddenly: it was said the illness was brought on by the drinking of coffee prepared in Beamish's house. Asked about this and the death of his wife brought no response from Beamish. Not surprisingly, he was found guilty of murder. Afterwards he complained to his gaolers saying that a 'clever barrister' would have got him off.

Beamish was visited regularly at Warwick Gaol by family and friends. On Christmas Eve his surviving two children were brought to see him. For this visit the governor allowed him to wear his normal clothes, but the visit took place at a different time and Beamish met the children in prison dress, his little girl initially not recognizing him. Beamish grabbed her in his arms and smothered her in kisses, the little girl responded by calling out, 'Dad, dah, Dad dah.' As he released her from his embrace the little girl grabbed at the black cloth, which bore his prison number and said, 'What dis, what dis, Dad dah.' For the first time since he was taken and tried Beamish showed emotion, and broke down and put his head against the wall and wept bitterly. Even the hardened prison guards were seen to cry.

On the Saturday he was paid a visit by his aged blind uncle who hoped that Beamish would confess to him – he did not. Then on the Sunday he attended a 'condemned sermon' in the gaol chapel and afterwards was visited by the Reverend Mr Baker who finally brought forth Beamish's admittance of guilt, which he wrote down on the morning of his execution. In it he said:

I cannot say more of the first cause of sickness of my children, God bless them ... but finding my wife was so ill, I was wicked enough to get the stuff. It was my hand that did the deed, and everyone else is innocent of it. I did repent of it as soon as done. But dare not say anything about it. God forgive me ...

Beamish also admitted verbally to the Reverend Mr Baker that it was he who had written the supposed suicide note.

There is a description from a booklet called, 'The Pistol, the Knife and the Poison Drug' published shortly after the execution of Beamish which was shared with another criminal, named Thompson. It records:

During the night large numbers of people had arrived in Warwick to witness the execution, but from three o'clock in the morning until ten o'clock, the hour appointed for the mournful event the throng was continuous. Though the concourse of spectators was not so large as generally expected. Their behaviour was of the most orderly character. There was a little good-natured crowding and pushing, and even laughter at the foot of the scaffold.

But the character of the crowd was somewhat superior to that which is generally present at such a spectacle. Its distinguishing characteristic was the number of decently dressed females, and the respectable appearance of a large number of the men. Without the slightest intimidation by the previous appearance of any official on the scaffold, Thompson stepped on with a firm tread, immediately followed by Beamish, equally firm. Both men took a strong steady look at the crowd. Smith the hangman, instantly drew their caps over their heads, the noose was placed round their necks. Smith and the turnkeys shook hands with them, there was a stepping back of the officials, the hangman drew the bolt, and both were launched into eternity. A few convulsive twitches and the whole scene, which did not occupy more than three minutes, was over.

It continues:

The Coventry bell-ringers were present at the execution and after it was over they went to St. Mary's Church ... and whilst the men were hanging, the eight bells of that church were ringing out a merry peal. It is charitable to suppose this was done for practice and not for any joyful manifestation for the death of Beamish.

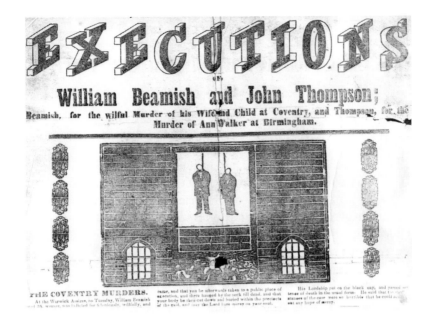

EXECUTIONS

William Beamish and John Thompson;
Beamish, for the wilful Murder of his Wife and Child at Coventry, and Thompson, for the Murder of Ann Walker at Birmingham.

THE COVENTRY MURDERS.

Execution broadside sold at Warwick and Coventry on the day of Beamish's execution. Coventry City Libraries, Local Studies

It is believed around 4,000 witnessed the execution and it was noted that unusually no baked potato men were present. While waiting the crowd growing impatient, swayed about, causing large waves and occasionally hoisted someone onto their heads and passed them across the crowds to the gallows and back; much like a modern pop concert. It was noted by other sources that Beamish being a lighter man did not die instantly, 'there being a strange tremor of the limbs and body' taking him nearly half a minute to meet his end.

The crowd quickly began to disperse while men and women dashed amongst them selling copies of execution broadsides, such as, 'The Sorrowful Lament of William Beamish'. It is said many went to the shop of Mr Findlow in Jury Street to see a photographic portrait of William Beamish, which was exhibited to raise money for his two children. After hanging for the usual time the bodies of Beamish and Thompson were returned to Warwick Gaol where they were soon buried. The hangman is said to have left the scene quickly in a gig, and not by train as at the previous execution, when the hangman had been mobbed like a pop star.

CHAPTER 18

Child Murder in Whitmore Park 1862

O n 16 May 1862 an inquest was held at the *Rose* public house in Lockhurst Lane on the remains of nineteen-month-old Harriet Marston who had been found drowned in a local pit the previous day. The first witness called by Arthur Carter the coroner was 15-year-old William Payne who said:

> *I live in Carpenter's Lane, Foleshill and am a weaver. The deceased child, Harriet Marston is my half sister ... she lived with us. Her father's name is John Marston ... He is my father-in-law* [William referred to his step father as his father-in-law throughout the trial and often referred to his new step-sister as, the child or 'it']. *The deceased was the only child, which my mother had by the prisoner. They were married two years last Christmas.*

After this the inquest was adjourned till the following day so a post mortem could be carried out on the body.

The *Coventry Standard* reported that at the recommencement of the trial, 'John Marston, father of the deceased child, was present, in custody and seemed to be labouring under the same stupefied and bewildering semi-consciousness which was so apparent at the former sitting.'

Marston's stepson resumed giving evidence saying:

> *On the morning of the 8th inst. I left home to go to work at about half past eight o'clock. At that time my father-in-law and deceased were not up. I returned at 1 o'clock to my dinner and learned that that they had been away from home several hours. I went to work again until six o'clock the same evening.*
>
> *My father-in-law had not returned with the child; and I heard that he was supposed to have made away with it, and at the solicitation of my mother I went to Coventry to a person named*

Adkins ... to ask if he knew anything of the child. Mr Adkins said he had not seen either of them.

When asked about his stepfather's relationship with the child, William Payne said he was passionately fond of her, and was always afraid that she should be hurt. He added that he was always in the habit of taking the child on walks around the fields. The second witness was John Shaw, a labourer who lived in Holbrooks. He did not personally know Marston but said that on the day, 'between ten and eleven o'clock I was ploughing by the side of the foot-road near the Jack-pit leading to the pit where the body was found.'

He continued:

I see the man now in custody. He is the same person who passed me that day. He had a female child in his arms at the time. He walked on to the swing gate near the Jack-pit, and sat down for about twenty minutes, nursing the child. He afterwards got up, carrying the child in his arms at that time. He seemed to be very fond of the child, from the manner he seemed to be talking to it. He stood by while the horses passed and called the child's attention to them in a kind manner.

The next statement came from Police Constable William Miller who stated, 'I was on duty in Whitmore Park ... in a field called Ox Close ... I saw the prisoner with a female child ... near the pit ...' Another police constable, Joseph Knight then stated:

From information received ... I went to the Prince William Henry *public house, Foleshill, where I found the prisoner, his wife, and the landlady of the house Mrs. Ward. They were standing in*

'He walked past the Jack Pit ... nursing the child.'

*the passage when I went there. We all went into the parlour. The
mother of the deceased asked him where the child was, and he
made no reply. I also asked him the same question, but he did not
answer me. He appeared to be in great trouble, and I asked his
wife and Mrs. Ward to leave the room. They did so, and he
voluntarily told me that he had tied some worsted round the
child's body, attached a stone to it, put some flowers in its left
hand and thrown it into the pit … He also pointed out to me
where the pit was …*

Police Constable Knight then charged John Marston with the
wilful murder of his own child and later returned with
Inspector Welch to make an unsuccessful search of the pit. On
the following morning they returned with other officers and
began dragging the pit with a grappling iron. Hours passed
before the body was eventually hooked and dragged to the
surface still weighed down by the heavy stone.

Dr Phillips, surgeon said of his examination of the remains,
'I found it to be the body of a very healthy, highly developed
and well nourished child. There was not the slightest mark of
external violence, nor evidence of internal disease, nor
anything to cause death except for suffocation by drowning.'
Queries were made to the state of Marston's mind and a
verdict of 'Wilful Murder' quickly brought.

The Prince William Henry *on the Foleshill Road where Marston was arrested.*
Gordon Cowley

A re-examination of John Marston took place in Coventry's County Hall, before the Reverend Mr Lickorish, A H Pears and E Phillips, and caused great public interest. Marston, it is said, now appeared to be more conscious of the enormity of his crime, he stood in the dock, his eyes red from crying, but still had that air about him of bewilderment.

The examination began when Inspector Welch read out the statement he had taken from Marston after his initial arrest; it said:

I live in Carpenter's Lane [later Station Street West], *Foleshill; this morning at about eleven o'clock, I threw my little girl into a pit on Mr. Berry's farm in Whitmore Park. I tied a stone to her with some worsted; she is in a pit, which has been fresh cleared out. I will show you the place, if you will go with me. Her name is Harriet Marston, she is about eighteen months old.*

He continued, 'I did not do it on her account, but my wife's. I threw her into the pit over the footpath. I think it was the second field in the road going from Mr. John Berry's house.' Inspector Welch then told the court that Marston was searched and found to be carrying two pocket knives, a pair of scissors, cord, string and silk thread, and afterwards he left with Knight to search the pit. On his return Marston asked if he had found the girl, to which he replied, 'No we have not.' Marston then said, 'I can show you where she is, to a few feet,' and Welch agreed to take him the next morning.

Welch then described to the court what had taken place the following morning. On the road to Foleshill, Marston suddenly began to talk, saying: 'I little thought I should have done this; my trouble has been very great. When anything is amiss at home my wife encourages her children [including William Payne, by a previous marriage] to do as they like. If I attempt to correct them, then she is angry with me.' Marston then held his head in his hands and began crying, saying, 'She has been my sole care; she has occupied all my thoughts, when I have been from home and I thought if anything happened to me, then they would throw their spite at her. I loved her from the moment she came into the world.'

Inspector Welch then said:

We then came to a place on the bank near a stile, where someone appeared to have been sitting down on the grass, and some flowers lay about. He then became very much affected and rested his head upon the stile. He was so much affected that I allowed him to indulge his feelings four or five minutes, before getting over the stile. When he did so he pointed at some fragments of flowers and grass that lay on the ground, which he said the child had been playing with. At the next stile he again became very much affected. He was then in sight of the pit where the body was found … The prisoner went up to the hedge adjoining it and crying very much, he pointed to a part of the water, and said, 'She lies just there.'

The body was found where Marston indicated and Welch held up the stone in court which had held the child in her watery tomb. The court committed Marston to trial for 'wilful murder.' During the time of his confinement in Coventry Gaol the gaol had been closed and the prisoners transferred to Warwick. John Marston was finally put on trial in August at Warwick assizes. Marston swayed the jury with his remorse and the fact that he thought he was in some way protecting his much loved little girl, from the hatred of his wife and adopted family. The jury sympathized with the sad creature that stood before them and John Marston was acquitted on the grounds of insanity.

CHAPTER 19

The Gosford Street Murder
1871

The *Coventry Herald and Free Press* reported that on Wednesday, 6 December 1871:

a murder of a very shocking nature ... was committed in Gosford Street, Coventry. The circumstances so far as we are able to ascertain them, appear to be these. The murdered man, whose name was John Millward, was an overlooker at Leigh Mills, Coventry and resided with his mother, a widow in Gosford Street, in this city.

Brown stabbing Millward in Gosford Street as depicted in a nineteenth-century Penny Dreadful. Coventry Evening Telegraph

He was about eighteen years of age. The murderer is a young man of about the same age, named Arthur Frederick Brown, who was until a fortnight ago, also employed at Leigh Mills.

In consequence however of some irregularity, he was discharged. For this he seems to have blamed Millward, although in point of fact, the latter had nothing to do with it. It is however beyond doubt that he was considerably irritated at receiving his discharge and that he and Millward were together on Wednesday evening in Gosford Street, close to the deceased's home, though how the meeting originated has not yet been explained.

It seems that first knowledge of the event came at six-thirty when the wife and apprentice of a grocer, David Brown, heard a shout from outside. This was immediately followed by John Millward staggering from the entry to the court where he lived to the other side of the street. As he lay dying Millward told the first person to reach him that Brown had stabbed him in the heart and within seconds Brown himself was seen to run off down the street towards Gosford Bridge. Dr Brown was called for and Millward was carefully carried home where he died.

The press continued their report of the event by pointing out that:

Brown kept company at last Coventry Fair with a young woman named Martha Waters, who, however, has since then refused his society. This he seems to have taken badly, and to have cherished angry feelings towards the girl, and also to the young man with whom now she is consorting. On Wednesday Martha Waters received a note from Brown, purporting to have been written by her present sweetheart, and asking her to meet him near her home in Fleet Street. The note had been handed to her by the deceased, at Leigh Mills, where she is also employed. In doing so Millward remarked that it was from Brown, and advised her to beware of him, saying that he carried a pistol.

In consequence of this warning, the young woman took with her a companion, and waited for Brown at the spot and time named – the hour appointed, singularly enough being the same as that in which the murder took place. He, however did not make his appearance; but it is conjectured, with some reason, that his intentions towards her were of a sinister kind, and that he probably intended to do her serious bodily harm, if not take away her life.

It appears in the time leading up to this event that Brown, who lived with his mother at 10 Jesson Street, had been living away from home, and for the several hours that he was 'wanted' on Wednesday night the police could not discover where he was. He was finally discovered in bed during the early hours of 7 December at a house in Chauntry Place. Police Sergeant Sheasby made the arrest with two officers and Brown came quietly saying that he was sorry for what had happened as he was in a 'passion,' because Millward had, 'taunted me so'. The police officers collected up the bloodstained pocket knife, which had been used in the murder, and also found a loaded pistol and a quantity of ammunition.

Later that morning he was brought before magistrates at the Police Court, and was there remanded until the police gathered further evidence. The inquest itself took place at the County Hall a few days later. The first witness was Frederick Wimbush, the grocer's apprentice, who testified that he had heard the words, 'You damn scamp, I'll have you locked up tomorrow morning.' Wimbush saw Brown run down the street and said Millward, 'came across the street to the shop window.

He then pulled back his coat and I saw the blood running from his left side. He said that Arthur or Albert Brown had stabbed him … He afterwards said he was dying and I put my arms round him to support him. Mrs Brown told me to take him to the *Fox and Vivian* to give him some brandy. I attempted to take him but after walking about a yard he was unable to go any farther. Several people afterwards came and he was carried home …'

Ann Peel testified that she had seen Millward in Gosford Street

The County Hall, Coventry where Millward's inquest took place.

shortly before the incident, and then a woman had come running saying a man had been stabbed. Peel said, 'I ran to see who it was and found Millward on his knees on the road. I spoke to him, and asked what was the matter – he knows me, and called me by my name three times. He said, "O dear, Annie, I've been stabbed to the heart." I asked him who did it and he said it was Arthur Brown, I asked him why he did it, and he said, "I got him the sack." Peel then asked Millward if he and Brown had had words, but Millward said not: Brown had been quite collected and knew what he was doing.

This was followed by the testimonies of numerous people identifying Brown as the man seen at and leaving the scene of the crime. Police Sergeant Sheasby testified saying that on the night of his arrest, Brown had asked if Millward was seriously hurt. Sheasby replied he was but did not mention the fact that he was dead until he charged Brown with murder at the police station in St Mary's Street.

Dr Brown then gave evidence and said: 'I found him lying on the floor, in a room down stairs and breathing, but pulseless. I gave him brandy at once, and examined his chest, and found a wound about three quarters of an inch ... between the fifth and sixth rib, on the left side ... in a few minutes he was extinct.' The doctor then read out a detailed description of the post mortem, which he performed on the body with a fellow surgeon. He concluded that: 'Death is the result of the wound (through the walls of the chest) to the important vital organs contained in the cavity ...'

Jane Hewitt, who also worked at Leigh Mills, knew both men, and said she and a friend had met Brown in the *Burges* back on 20 November and had walked towards the circus, which had been performing in the city at the time. At that time Brown's animosity towards Millward was clear, for he said, 'I have had my knife in him for some time, and shall have my revenge upon him yet'. The jury retired for only a few minutes before returning a charge of wilful murder. Brown was committed to trial at the next assizes at Warwick County Court.

The trial took place at the Warwick Winter Assizes held on 20 December 1871 and the case was presided over for the Crown by the Hon. Chandos Leigh of Stoneleigh Abbey and Mr William Dugdale of Polesworth. All previous witnesses

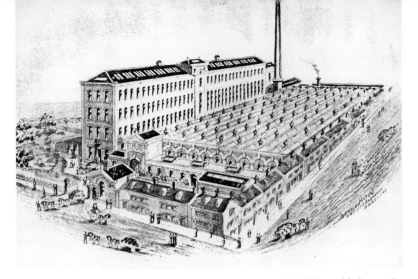

Leigh Mills in Hill Street where both men worked. Lord Leigh presided over the inquest.

appeared and little new evidence was given other than that from Alfred Saunders, an overlooker at Leigh Mills. Saunders had suspended Brown for failing to return to work after being given time off when he claimed to be looking after his sick mother. However, shortly before he was taken for the murder his mother said he had not been staying at home lately. Asked if John Millward, who had recently become an overlooker under him, had said anything to him regarding Brown that might have led to his dismissal, Saunders replied that Millward had said nothing, and this was later confirmed by another witness. Saunders testified that he had not wished Brown to lose his job, but intended him to be reprimanded, however Brown did not return. Although Brown claimed he was off work to look after his sick mother, Saunders was told that he had been seen at Eaves Music Hall one night. Saunders, therefore, had wanted Brown's excuse checked out. When told that he had been seen, Brown replied, 'I know who told you that, it was Millward.' Saunders told him that was untrue.

Henry Benson, a weaver, was next called and said he spoke to Brown on the 23 November, and asked him when he would be returning to work, to which Brown replied, 'I am not going back at all for John Millward has got me the sack, and I will kill him for it. I have owed him a grudge for a long while, and I mean to pay it.'

A letter was then read out written by Brown during his confinement in Warwick Gaol. It said:

My dear Mrs. Millward, I write to you asking for forgiveness for killing my last companion, John. I have repented ever since I done it. I pray night and morning for my sins, and also for John, and for you, for the Lord to keep you up in your trouble. I have your feelings as well as my own. I did not think what I was doing when I done it, and, if I should get over this, I will think it my duty to do all that lies in my power, and give you as much as I can out of my wages. Forgive me. I think it has not only caused trouble, between you and me, but others. Forgive me, I asked you once more, or I shall not rest happy.

Mr Bristowe then gave an eloquent speech on behalf of the prisoner in which he appealed to the jury for a lesser verdict of manslaughter. He said that despite the testimonies that had been presented, there was no positive evidence that the prisoner had deliberately slain John Millward, 'with malice aforethought'. This was perhaps not strictly true as Brown had stated before the murder that, 'I have had my knife in him for some time, and shall have my revenge on him yet', although, of course, this did not necessarily mean he intended to kill him.

Mr Bristowe, having brought forward witnesses who had seen Brown standing openly in the street, argued that if he had intended to commit a crime he would have hidden in the darkness of the entry. Sergeant Sheasby said his conduct upon his arrest suggested he had committed an unpremeditated act, and not wilful murder. That said, Brown was unaware when he was taken that Millward was dead. Finally, Dr Brown testified and when questioned agreed that the deathblow could have been struck in self-defence. However, this could not be proved, as the only witness of the incident was dead.

Lord Leigh summed up for the Crown going into the smallest detail, and he pointed out the salient points that showed the motive and intention of the prisoner. Such evidence, he said, clearly eliminated any possibility of manslaughter. The jury retired and returned in five minutes with a verdict of guilty, but added a plea for mercy because of Brown's age and previous good character.

Lord Leigh then assumed the black cap and addressed Brown saying it was not only murder legally, but the defendant had nursed his feelings of revenge for some time, and this was, therefore, a premeditated and intentional act. He added that he hoped the prisoner would continue in the vein of the letter with prayer and repentance adding finally, 'I hope and pray that you find salvation.' He then pronounced the formal sentence of death upon Brown who stood in tears between two warders. He was taken down in a state of great agitation while family members sobbed in the gallery.

While Brown sat in Warwick Gaol under sentence of death, some were fighting behind the scenes for a reduction of the capital sentence to one of life imprisonment. On 12 January 1872 the *Herald* reported:

> *The efforts made to obtain a reprieve of Arthur Frederick Brown, recently convicted of the murder of John Millward in Gosford Street, have proved successful. Late on Saturday evening a messenger from the Home Office arrived at Warwick Gaol, and handed to the Governor the formal document announcing this result. On the intelligence being communicated to Brown he received it with great manifestations of joy, and shed tears …*
>
> *The same edition of the paper contained the result of an appeal it had made previously for John Millward's mother, 'whose future lot must certainly be a hard, up-hill struggle with the world, as she will have to maintain herself and her five children, under 14 years of age'. The appeal brought in a total of £82. 6s. 9d, with money coming in from various individuals, reading like a Coventry Who's Who, such as Lord Leigh, John Gulson, John Rotherham and Thomas Cash, to name but a few.*

The broadside publisher did not lose out on the fact that Millward was not hanged and composed a song instead on the, 'Dreadful Murder of John Millward'.
Coventry City Libraries, Local Studies

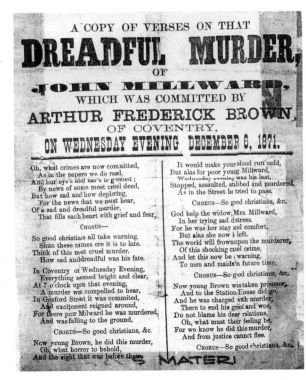

A COPY OF VERSES ON THAT

DREADFUL MURDER,

OF

JOHN MILLWARD,

WHICH WAS COMMITTED BY

ARTHUR FREDERICK BROWN,

OF COVENTRY,

ON WEDNESDAY EVENING DECEMBER 6, 1871.

Oh, what crimes are now committed,
As in the papers we do read,
And bur eye's and ear's is greeted ;
By news of some most cruel deed.
But how sad and cruel murder,
For the news that we must hear,
Of a sad and dreadful murder,
That fills each heart with grief and fear,

CHORUS—

So good christians all take warning.
Shun these crimes ere it is to late.
Think of this most cruel murder,
How sad and dreadful was his fate.

In Coventry on Wednesday Evening,
Everything seemed bright and clear,
At 7 o'clock upon that evening,
A murder was compelled to hear,
In Gosford Street it was commited,
And excitement reigned around,
For there poor Milward he was murdered,
And was falling to the ground.

CHORUS—So good christians, &c.

Now young Brown, he did this murder,
Oh, what horror to behold,
And the sight that was before them,

It would make your blood run cold,
But alas for poor young Millward,
Wednesday evening was his last,
Stopped, assaulted, stabbed and murdered,
As in the Street he tried to pass.

CHORUS—So good christians, &c.

God help the widow, Mrs. Millward,
In her trying sad distress.
For he was her stay and comfort,
But alas she now i left.
The world will frown upon the murderer,
Of this shocking cruel crime,
And let this now be a warning,
To men and maids in future time.

CHORUS—So good christians, &c.

Now young Brown was taken prisoner,
And to the Station House did go,
And he was charged with murder,
There to end his grief and woe,
Do not blame his dear relations,
Oh, what must their feeling be,
For we know he did this murder,
And from justice cannot flee.

CHORUS—So good christians, &c.

CHAPTER 20

Salvation and Murder: Kirby House
1887

n the 5 August 1887 the *Coventry Herald* informed the good citizens of Coventry of yet another murder:

Yesterday morning a great sensation was caused in Coventry by the report that a young woman had been murdered. Enquiry revealed the fact that the report unfortunately had too real a foundation. It appears that for several years past a man named Thomas Payne and his wife Maria have been living at number 16, Little Park Street, as caretakers of the office of Messrs. Troughton, Lea and Kirby, solicitors. Mrs Payne's sister, a young [twenty-three-year-old] woman named Charlotte Taylor, has also been living with them, her services being utilized in the work of caretaking. Some time ago Payne was a regular attendant at the services of the Salvation Army, but for some reason he severed his connection with that organisation, and conceived a violent hatred for it, and even went so far as to abuse and threaten one of the officers, now residing at a distance.

The cause of the estrangement is not clear; but it is stated that formerly the deceased had lived in a state of concubinage with Payne, and that on her becoming a member of the Salvation Army she resolved to terminate their relationship. The anger which he felt at her attitude was deepened when he made the discovery that recently she had commenced a correspondence with a male member of the army out of Coventry.

The 'concubinage' the press talks about between Payne and Taylor appears to have lasted for about four years. When Taylor became pregnant Maria Payne (her sister) accused her husband, Thomas Payne, of being the father. To which it is said he replied, 'If you accuse me of that I will run a knife through you.' Afterwards Taylor refused to name the father and it was thought that Payne had threatened her into silence. Later Charlotte Taylor

Kirby House, Little Park Street, scene of the murder.

became close to Leonard Doy, a lieutenant in the Salvation Army and corresponded with him when he was moved from Coventry. Payne became aware of the letters and two days before the murder had an argument with his wife concerning them, in which he accused her and Taylor of deceiving him by pretending there were no letters. During the argument it is said that Payne threatened that somebody's blood would fly for it, saying to his wife, 'I shall not take your life and I shan't tell you who the person may be.'

That day he followed Taylor as she attended a number of services and as she left he persisted in haranguing her and trying to get her to take off the bonnet and leave the army. That evening he met her as she returned from the Salvation Factory and asked her to come home, but when she discovered that her sister was not there she ran away. While searching for her Payne met his wife and returned home with her, but his threats and violence towards her were such that she felt obliged to go and report it to the police. Payne went out in search of his wife but met Taylor and again induced her to return home, which she did. Once in the house Payne locked the door and removed the key, Taylor ran for the back door, Payne ran after her and while struggling with her tore the army bonnet from her head. That night she stayed with another Salvationist, Mrs Molesworth, and told her sister who was there what had occurred.

On the Monday Mrs Payne and Taylor returned to Little Park Street and a reconciliation was achieved. Shortly afterwards Payne wrote an abusive and threatening letter to Leonard Doy. On the Tuesday Payne again returned to the subject of the letters, and reproached Taylor for giving her heart to Doy. On the following day he wrote a second letter to Doy that accused him of rank hypocrisy in claiming to be a godly man while he encouraged Taylor to do wrong. He told Doy he had burnt all the letters and he would never see Charlotte Taylor again. Payne also wrote a ranting letter to General Booth.

On that Wednesday Payne appeared to be in a sound state of mind as he had held a lengthy conversation with one of the partners of the practice. On Thursday morning Payne woke his wife up saying, 'Maria, get up and see the light shine in for the last time.' Charlotte Taylor had prepared breakfast, Payne sat and ate it and said to her, 'This is the last breakfast we shall have together. If General Booth only knew what was going to happen it would pay him to take us all into the army work.' He looked across the table and added to his wife, 'Maria, if you only knew what is going to happen you would consent to anything.'

Breakfast was quickly finished in silence and Taylor left to do her work. Payne followed soon after taking a large table knife with him. What happened next was reported in the *Herald*, it reads:

> *Taylor was dusting one of the offices, and Payne, going up to her from behind, it is supposed, took, hold of her hair and drawing back her head, attempted to cut her throat. She struggled for life, and took hold of the weapon with her left hand, and a number of slight cuts were inflicted on her face and neck. Payne then wrenched the knife violently through her hand, and cut it so badly that it became useless, and afterwards drawing the knife across her throat, he inflicted the fatal wound. The head was half severed from the body.*

Payne's wife was carrying water downstairs and heard a strange gurgling sound coming from the room. She ran to the front door opened it and screamed, 'Murder.' She then went back inside and from the bottom of the stairs called Charlotte

Payne murdering Taylor in the upstairs backroom of Kirby House.

six times. No answer came and then, Thomas Payne called out, 'Maria! Charlotte's dead. I've murdered her and it is all ended.' Maria Payne, in a hysterical state, ran from the house to the police station in St Mary's Street, where she was greeted by Inspector Wyatt. He eventually calmed her down enough to make sense of what she was saying, and then realized Payne was standing nearby. Payne spoke calmly saying, 'If you go into Little Park Street you'll see what's the matter. I've murdered my wife's sister.' Payne remained calm and quiet all the time and was placed in the station yard under the eye of Constable Sale.

Meanwhile Inspector Wyatt accompanied by Police Constable Spicer headed for nearby Little Park Street and found Charlotte Taylor lying dead on the office floor bearing a cut from two inches below one ear to the same distance from the other. Soon after they moved the body upstairs and later to the mortuary at the Coventry and Warwickshire Hospital.

Wyatt told Payne he would be charged with the murder to which he replied, 'It's quite right.' Payne was then locked up but not before a doctor was brought to check his finger which he had cut while doing the dastardly deed.

On the same morning Payne was brought before the City Police Court and charged with maliciously murdering Charlotte Taylor. He was described as a thirty-eight-year-old labourer, middle height, of 'spare habit' and with thin face, sandy whiskers, beard and moustache, dark short hair and hollow eyes. He was placed in the dock and stood apparently gazing without concern at the bench.

Payne identified himself and Inspector Wyatt told the court of what happened saying that:

We went upstairs and on the first floor in the back office I found the body of Charlotte Taylor lying on her back on the floor in a pool of blood. We examined her and formed the opinion she was quite dead at the time. The woman had her throat cut very badly. At the same time I found the knife produced lying close to the body, under her right arm. I sent police constable Spicer for a doctor ...

The mayor Alderman Thomson asked Payne if there was any reason he should not be remanded, Payne replied, 'No' and he was remanded accordingly.

The official inquest was opened the next day in the Justice Room (the Old Mayoress's Parlour) in St Mary's Hall. The coroner Dr Charles Iliffe called only for such evidence as was necessary for the purpose of registering the victim for burial.

Payne's wife Maria gave the evidence, saying, 'the deceased was my sister, and is 23 years of age, and is the daughter of William Taylor, gardener, of 174, Soho-road, Birmingham'.

At the Magistrates' Inquest Payne made a long and rambling statement saying that he was aggrieved at finding that Leonard Doy had visited Charlotte at the house in his absence and had afterwards corresponded with her. 'That's what has done it,' he said, 'There has been nothing but a parcel of lies, and nothing but a

The Justice Room (Old Mayoress's Parlour) set out for an inquest in the gatehouse of St Mary's Hall. This was the scene of many judicial inquests.
Coventry City Libraries, Local Studies

parcel of lies has placed me here.' Before committal Payne stated that he was going to maintain silence during the trial, he did not.

The inquest over, Payne was sent to Warwick Gaol to await trial, which began on 14 November 1887. The judge, Baron Huddleston informed the jury of the outline of events and added:

The motive perhaps, if a motive is required, is obvious and was discovered in some letters which the prisoner had written on the day before the crime was committed, to a person who was an officer in the Salvation Army ... it seems to me beyond all doubt that there had been some – perhaps I should not be justified in saying intimacy, but there certainly can be no doubt that there was a strong feeling on the part of the prisoner towards his wife's sister, and it seems that on those two days – the day before the murder and the day of the murder ... he had written letters, which will be laid before you, of a most violent and vindictive character ... and it seems in order to satisfy that horrible passion he had written these letters to this man and then perpetrated this deed ...

The trial resumed the following day and the press states that Payne stood in the dock looking in 'good health' and, 'stood stiffly, stolid and unmoved, with his head slightly tilted ... and his eyebrows resolutely knit ... His shoulders gave an occasional nervous shrug suggesting discomfort, but otherwise his character was remarkable.'

The Clerk read out the indictment against Payne and asked him if he was guilty or not guilty. Payne answered in a decisive manner, 'Guilty.' The clerk responded, 'You say you are guilty?' 'I am', he replied causing a sensation in the packed courtroom. There was a short delay and the judge asked him if with due reflection he still pleaded guilty, Payne asked him to repeat the question then replied, 'I do, my lord.' There was another brief pause as pleas were recorded and Payne stood indifferently in the dock. The judge then said, 'Thomas Payne, you stand capitally convicted of the crime of wilful murder upon your own confession. Have you anything to say now why sentence of death should not be passed upon you.' 'Nothing at all, Sir', Payne replied.

The judge placed on the black cap and in the stunned silence of the courtroom said:

Thomas Payne, you have pleaded guilty to almost the greatest offence known to the law and any persons who have read the depositions and knows the circumstances of this case cannot doubt but that you deliberately committed the crime to which you have pleaded guilty. The unfortunate person whose life you took was related to you by marriage. She was the sister of your wife and I am afraid it is too clear that she was the mother of a child by you, that these relations had ceased probably for some time, and that then when you found she was, as you thought receiving attentions from another man, the demoniacal feeling of jealousy operated upon your mind: and it is clear that for some short time prior to the execution of your threats that you contemplated killing that woman. The letters, which you wrote, are unmistakable signs of the wicked passion that was guiding your hand on the day ... you entered the room determined to take her life. You approached her from behind, put your hand round her and attempted to cut her throat, and after a vain struggle on her part, you accomplished your object ... It is sometimes usual when unhappy men actuated by strong feelings ... appear before a tribunal such as this, for their friends to offer for them the suggestion, that they were not in their right mind, but it can certainly not be put forward in your case ... and you seem at this moment conscious that you have deservedly forfeited your life ... The sentence of the court upon you is for the crime of wilful murder of which you are now convicted is that you be taken from the place where you are to the prison whence you came, and from thence on a day appointed that you be taken to a place of execution, and that you be hanged by the neck until your body is dead, and that your body when dead may be buried in the precinct of the prison from which you shall be confined. After this may the Lord have mercy upon your soul.

During the judge's delivery Payne stood with the same determined expression on his face, but occasionally closed his eyes while family members sobbed in the gallery. Just as the wardens were about to take him down Payne asked if he could

A courtroom scene at Warwick Assize around the time of Payne's trial.

speak, the request was granted and Payne with his eyes closed nearly the whole time said:

> *My Lord, I have to say this, that I have made my peace with God*
> *– I am guilty of killing Charlotte Taylor – that the evidence that*
> *has been given is very false indeed. I admit I wrote the letters to*
> *Leonard Doy, but when I wrote them I was in a state of*
> *excitement. I can declare before my God that I had no intention*
> *of taking the life of Charlotte Taylor, and as regards the evidence*
> *of my wife, I can look God in the face and say it is false, and it is*
> *on her behalf that I pleaded not guilty* [he meant to say guilty].
> *For if I had laid it before the court my dear wife would never have*

been able to have looked up again as long as she lived. God bless her this morning is my prayer. She hated me, and she has certainly been unfaithful and an untruthful wife to me, but God bless her ... I admit I killed her sister, I am sorry to have to stand in such a position. I have been a true, honest and faithful husband to my wife. May God bless her. I never was so speared in all my life as I was at the beginning of last April when I asked my wife a question. If she is here in court she will remember that I went down upon my knees, and I vowed I would be true and honest and faithful to her, and to my home, that I loved my home, and if she had loved me as I loved her I should not have been standing here. It is me that killed Charlotte Taylor but it is her sister that is her murderer.

At this point Taylor's tone became strong and he raised his arms to emphasize his words, saying, 'God bless her. I killed poor Charlotte, but it is her sister who has murdered her. Goodbye, God bless you all, for I may never see you anymore. I am parted from my wife, but it may not be forever.' He added, 'God have mercy upon me,' struck his chest and said, 'I am saved, thank God. Goodbye, my lord.'

The press reported these facts and added:

His reputation amongst his neighbours was that of an overbearing, bigoted man, not amenable to reason, nor willing to listen to any argument opposed to his own ... But if the stubbornness of the prisoner was remarkable, what shall be said of the extraordinary speech he addressed to the court? Without, as we believe, the slightest cause, he laid the blame for the crime on the head of his wife. Such an instance of cold bloodied, horrible cruelty to a harmless woman has, we venture to say, never been witnessed before in Warwick Assize Court. Unable to justify his own conduct, Payne, in the last words he will have the opportunity of addressing to the public, wilfully sought to ruin the character of the sister of the girl so foully murdered in August last. Doubtless he sees not the slightest chance of evading the extreme penalty of the law, and we cannot think that anyone will intercede on behalf of such a heartless wretch.

Payne's wife no doubt had insisted her husband stopped his obsession with her sister, possibly demanded it and Payne fuelled by jealousy did just that by killing her, then blamed his wife for forcing his hand.

As he awaited his execution Payne was visited as was usual by clergy and the day before the execution he was visited by his mother, brother, then wife and her other sister. It is said that he slept well on his last night, and Berry the executioner arrived in Warwick early that Monday afternoon. The *Herald* reported that, 'The apparatus was new nearly fifteen years ago, when the first execution within the precinct of the gaol took place, the unfortunate culprit on that occasion being Edward Hancock, the Priors Hardwick murderer.' The reporter then goes on to describe Berry the executioner in detail down to what he was wearing. Executioners in those days appeared to be extremely popular drawing crowds on their arrival.

Payne had risen at 6 am on the 5 December 1887, his last day; he refused his breakfast; he had not the stomach for it. Afterwards he was ministered by the Reverend Mr Gibson and the gaol chaplain who prepared him for what was to come. At eight o'clock precisely Berry entered the cell and pinioned Payne's arms. Payne then shook Berry's hand and said, 'God bless you, I hope to meet you in heaven.' Payne was taken to the drop and eight members of the press brought in to witness the event. The drop was a simple device consisting of a strong beam fixed to the wall on each side of a yard. The rope itself was long, with the noose actually laying on the trap door. It had previously hanged eight murderers.

The press reported:

Berry returned to the small shed which had been built across the yard in close proximity to the drop. In a very few moments the procession was formed and came from the shed in the following order: The Under Sheriff; the chaplain ... Payne (who had a haggard expression and whose quivering clasped hands indicated his fearfully nervous condition); the Governor of the Gaol; the Gaol surgeon; some wardens ... making the total number of spectators twenty. The executioner placed Payne where he was required to stand upon the drop. Berry then strapped the culprit round the ankles, drew a white cap over his face, and adjusted the rope, drawing it up at the back of the left ear with what looked like a leather washer ... and then with a quickness that was astonishing, Berry passed round to the steps in front and to the left of the prisoner and immediately drew the bolt, the drop falling with a terrible crash and the prisoner's body sinking out of sight, the tightened and momentary quivering of the rope being the only indications of the convulsive moments below. During the last few moments occupied by the executioner in doing the dreadful work, the voice of the chaplain was heard in prayer, and the culprit just before the drop fell uttered in tremulous tones; 'God bless my wife; God help her and save her soul. Receive my soul, O Lord, for Jesus' sake. My Jesus, My Jesus.' Berry gave the culprit a drop of seven feet. After the drop fell ... the eyes of the executioner were fixed upon the suspended body. Then the whole of the persons present were allowed to approach the pit and view the lifeless body hanging there, with the hands clasped in death. The executioner then stated that while the prisoner was being conducted along the passage to the place of execution he said, 'Jesus is by me, Jesus is with me.' The reporters then withdrew remarking upon the expedition and care with which the whole of the arrangements had been carried out.

The author of the above report then concluded by saying that he now realized that the man he had travelled from Coventry to Warwick with was Berry himself, saying: 'The incident is sufficient to show that persons travelling by rail occasionally get into singular company without having the slightest knowledge of the fact.' As for Thomas Payne, the Little Park Street Murderer, he was buried in the precincts of Warwick Gaol.

CHAPTER 21

The Stoke Park Murders 1906

S toke Park off the Binley Road has always been a quiet respectable cul-de-sac of Coventry. At the beginning of the twentieth century, it was still semi-rural with the gentleman's green being a genteel place where cricket was played on a Sunday afternoon. Nearby, carts and waggons still tightened their wheels in the cool water of the old Horse Pool, and children played in the open spaces around the Park and the Green.

This respectable façade of Edwardian Stoke was shattered in January 1906 when the following report appeared in the *Coventry Herald*:

> *On Saturday afternoon two shocking murders were brought to light at Hawthorne Cottage, Stoke Park, the residence of Mr. and Mrs. Richard Phillips, both of whom have been done to death in a most brutal manner. They were both elderly, the husband having attained the age of seventy-five, while his wife was sixty-nine. The particulars, as they became known, and were pieced together revealed one of the worst and cruellest murders of modern times, and not only in this district, where the greatest sensation has been caused, but throughout the whole country.*

Stoke Green opposite Stoke Park in 1906. Hawthorn Cottage was visible across the green. Chris Green

The murdered couple were discovered by Richard Shell the baker, who, if the couple were out, always looked for a note which would be placed in the pantry window. On Thursday, 11 January this usual custom had apparently been departed from as neither Mr and Mrs Phillips nor the note were present. Shell returned the following day again found no one at home and again there was no note. The Venetian blinds were also down making the house look unoccupied. It was again the same on Saturday and Shell and a friend suspecting something was amiss gained entry to the house.

Nothing appeared unusual downstairs, but when the men went to the upstairs bedroom a ghastly sight met their eyes. The *Herald* continues:

> *On the floor of a bedroom Mr. and Mrs. Phillips were lying dead … Both were in their night apparel. Mr. Phillips lay partly under the bed, in a quantity of blood, having been the victim of most brutal treatment. His head bore signs of frightful blows and his wife, if anything had been knocked about even worse. She was on the floor at the foot of the bed, almost in a sitting position, as her night clothes were caught on the iron rail at the foot of the bedstead … on her examination it was seen that she was gagged, for which purpose one of her own garments had been used. In her case too the wounds were terrible – she was only recognised by the lower part of her face – her skull being literally smashed, and it was clear a most formidable weapon had been used.*

The first on the scene after the discovery were the Chief Constable, Mr C Charsley, Detective Inspector Imber and other members of the detective staff. They quickly discovered that the house had been entered from the back, through the large pantry window. Inside the pantry the murderer or murderers had knocked over and broken a vegetable dish on the stone floor. They had made their way through the pantry, kitchen and front sitting room, into the hallway and up the stairs to the bedroom on the right, where the couple slept.

In the sitting room downstairs there was a calendar on the mantelpiece, one that would be changed every day. It read 10 January, so the couple had either been killed on the night of

Wednesday, 10 January or in the early hours of 11 January. The motive for the crime appeared to be robbery as the contents of a cash box and two drawers appear to have been taken. Those who knew the couple however informed the police that they kept little cash in the house.

Mary Phillips had lived in the house, built by her first husband Mr Waterfall, for many years, then after his death spent five years on her own before marrying Richard Phillips in 1904. The press reported that: 'Mr. and Mrs. Phillips were not only held in esteem by those who to whom they were known in Stoke Park, but they could also claim many acquaintances and friends in other parts of the city.' The couple were often seen out walking together and appeared to be very happy, living comfortably off an income which they received periodically. Their neighbour Mrs Woodward told the press that she and Mrs Phillips had been great friends for more than twenty years, and often wandered into each other's houses. It was added, 'She had never known Mrs Phillips happier than during the last year; in fact she had confessed she had never been happier in her life than since her marriage to Mr. Phillips.' Prior to the marriage she had told Mrs. Woodward that she could not live through another winter alone.

On the Saturday night an ambulance came and the bodies were taken to the Workhouse Infirmary, Gulson Road to await the inquest. As news spread thousands came to Stoke Park to view the house and many 'camerists' photographed the building from the outside.

The inquest began on the Tuesday morning in the Board Room of the Workhouse mainly for the formal identification to allow burial. Mr Phillips's son identified his body and Robert Taylor, a first cousin of Mrs Phillips, who we will here more of later, formally identified her. Taylor was then asked when he last saw her to which he replied, that he last saw her alive the previous summer on Stoke Green, where they had a chat. It was then inquired if Mrs Phillips was, 'talkative or secretive in money matters'. To which he replied, 'Very quiet as a rule, but otherwise very lively and talkative.' The inquest was then adjourned to await further police evidence. The couple's funeral took place on the Wednesday and because of the vast crowds admission into the cemetery was by ticket only. The funeral was organized and attended by Robert Taylor.

The inquiry was led by Inspector Imber who had photographs of fingerprints from a whisky bottle found on the premises sent to Scotland Yard for checking; they however proved to belong to Mr Phillips. Another set found on the cash box, frustratingly, were impossible to photograph. No other fingerprints were found which suggested that the murderer wore gloves. It was reported that on the Thursday morning a man had gone to the police station and claimed to know who had committed the crime. However, within a short time he had three fainting fits and it was consequently thought he was, 'unhinged'. His evidence, however, was checked and found to be without foundation. The Police Surgeon suggested the man was a little unbalanced and should spend a few days in the Workhouse, which he did.

By late January the press were reporting that the police were struggling to find clues and those they had proved useless. There was talk that the murderer may not be found. In the house a rag was found on which the killer had wiped the blood from his hands; also a cycle lamp was found on the kitchen table, which had been converted to a dark lantern. This could not be linked to Mr and Mrs Phillips, and the police believed, therefore, that it must have been left by the murderer. They also believed the criminal was not a professional burglar as burglars did not normally murder their victims, but was someone who was concerned about being identified.

During an extensive search of the building the police found just over £16 in cash hidden in a bag in 'tree-pots' in the back of the building, upstairs, which was entirely built of glass like a greenhouse. Knowing the couple kept little ready cash it was now believed that this was their safe place for money and that the cash box had in fact contained little money. The only thing known to be definitely missing was a pocket watch, so it seemed that the person who had apparently killed them for their possessions had left practically empty handed. The police issued posters and a handbill that described the murder and gave detailed descriptions of the lamp and the watch. In

February a reward of £25 was offered for any person who could lead to the detection of the perpetrator or perpetrators of the murder.

The police continued their search in vain, even dragging the local ponds for clues. The crime had not only had an effect on Stoke but also the whole area. People were concerned that it could happen again and, because of new fears of the darkness, it was pointed out that Stoke Park and much of the city had few streetlights. It was decided in a full Council meeting that more lights, especially at Stoke Park, were needed to allay people's concerns.

On 17 March 1906 the *Coventry Herald* excitedly reported:

The Coventry Police investigation into the Stoke murders have ... brought up a man charged with the double crime, Charles Ernest Robert Taylor, a young carpenter of 16, Spencer Street, who was already in custody for a less grave offence. Taylor had in fact been arrested in connection with a stolen cycle the lamp of which had been found at the murder scene. Taylor was conveyed to Coventry from Warwick Gaol, in charge of a warder, who accompanied him to the dock ... He was driven from the railway station to the police court in an omnibus, and of course was visible en route, this having the effect of attracting a large number of people to St. Mary's Street. The court was almost filled, before the doors were opened, so that few among the waiting crowd outside were able to get admission. The proceedings did not last more than ten minutes, as the prosecution were not in a position to proceed that day ...

Inspector Imber was called and when asked if he had evidence that linked Taylor to the killing of Richard and Mary Phillips, he replied, 'Yes Sir.' Asked whether the police enquiries were completed, he said 'No Sir.' Taylor is said to have remained composed, showing no nerves. He stared either straight in front of him or looked aside to the clerk and Inspector Imber. When he was remanded he protested his innocence, in a voice described as, 'though pitched somewhat high, ... quite free from agitation'. What the press did not note at the time was that Robert Taylor was Mary Phillips's first cousin: the man who had

Spencer Street, Hillfields where Taylor lived with his parents. Coventry City Libraries, Local Studies

identified her body, organized the funeral and helped his father, another carpenter, make the coffins.

The following Saturday Taylor again appeared before the Police Court, and the public were aware of this and assembled en masse in St Mary's Street and Bayley Lane. He stood, 'self possessed and cool', before fifty witnesses and at one point scanned the public gallery and nodded to a couple of friends. Mr Parfitt, the prosecutor, spent ninety-five minutes outlining the case against Taylor and told the court of the cycle lamp found in the kitchen on the discovery of the murder. This lamp, he said, could be traced to a cycle in Taylor's possession. The court was told that Mary Phillips had been attacked first, then, when her husband tried to stop the attack, he too received many blows from some sort of instrument like a jemmy.

The prosecutor said that Taylor was short of work and seriously short of money. In his home they had discovered a summons to appear before the County Court because of money problems. He also said he would call before the bench a witness who had worked with Taylor and had had a conversation with him the previous year about his own financial difficulties. Taylor suggested he try burglary and even showed him how to open a window with a chisel. Another point brought up concerned two tools Taylor had had specially made recently, about eighteen inches long with curved ends.

Taylor was taken through this side door into the courtroom in St Mary's Street/Bayley Lane.

One of these tools was taken back as Taylor wanted it to be made into a cold chisel. Taylor had refused to say where the other tool was, and the prosecutor made the point that:

> *the instrument used in doing these poor people to death was an instrument which from its description by Thomas Eales* [the maker] *might as the doctor would tell them, have accounted for the peculiar character of the wounds that both these people manifested ... The importance of the case was this, that they were tools of a sufficient length to account for the terrible blows inflicted.*

The prosecutor also pointed out to the court the prisoner's strange conduct on the day of the murder. They could trace his movements for most of the day, beginning at three o'clock when he went into the workshop of Thomas Eales and fired a revolver. Eales, a long time friend, then went with Taylor to the *Alma Inn* and Taylor bought him a beer and tried to pay for it strangely in farthings. Between four and four-thirty Taylor appeared drunk at an unspecified 'works' and between six and seven he was at a factory in Harnall Lane, still very drunk and was thrown off the premises. Between nine and ten-fifteen he was playing darts at the *Woolpack* in Spon Street. He then visited a man named Charles Jordan at the back of Dresden's Tailors in Cross Cheaping and told him he was going to a club in Little Park Street. When later questioned about this by Inspector Imber, Taylor swore he had gone home and was in bed by eleven-thirty. Taylor's parents, however, testified that their son did not come home that night and returned the following morning in a wretched condition.

Another witness was one Benjamin Taylor who on the morning after the murder around 4.20 am, was on his way to work at Alfred Herbert's when he saw two men coming away from the direction of the cottage. On seeing him they immediately turned around and disappeared. Benjamin Taylor had also previously without hesitation picked out Charles Taylor from a police line up as one of the two men. Another

Dresden's tailor shop in Cross Cheaping next to the Talbot Inn. *Here Taylor visited Charles Jordan on the night of the murder.*

witness, a farmer named Boneham was going to his farm on the Walsgrave Road and saw a man around the same time. On reaching where the footpath from the Binley Road reached the Walsgrave Road he was passed by a man and bid him goodnight and the man wished him the same. Boneham also identified Taylor from a line up as being the man he had seen.

So Taylor was linked by witnesses' evidence to the area. Another important clue was, of course, the cycle lamp. It appears that in 1903 a Mr Johnstone of the Vernon Cycle Company made a cycle for a young man named John Lamont of Walsgrave and it was claimed the lamp from that cycle was the lamp found in the kitchen. On the 16 September 1905 the cycle had been left in the yard of the *Star Inn* and was stolen. Johnstone had told the police that he had visited the workshop of Thomas Henry Eales, and saw Taylor talking to Eales about a dismantled cycle that lay nearby. This Jonestone swore was the one he had built for John Lamont. Eales would later claim that Taylor had sold him the bike and he sold it on to Harry Lester of Spon Lane.

Later Lamont and his brother would both testify that the lamp found in Hawthorn Cottage belonged to that cycle, as it bore marks they could identify. Two discs of paper were pasted inside it to make it a dark lantern. Paper of the same type was found in Eales's workshop and experts testified that it matched chemically and by texture. The lamp had also been roughly japanned and japanning of the same quality and type was found in Eales's workshop. Also the wick found in the lamp was not of the type normally found in cycles. It was thicker and coarser than normal, had a streak of indigo blue running through it and had to be bent to fit. The same type was again found at Eales workshop.

The lamp was shown by Inspector Imber to Taylor's mother who immediately 'swooned.' When she came around the lamp was shown to the father who appeared to nearly faint. Taylor was then told that his mother when asked previously had said that she had seen the lamp in her house. Taylor replied, 'Oh, she's mistaken; she's thinking of another lamp I sold to a man named Newey.' It was however pointed out that the lamp in Mr Newey's possession was completely different from the lamp in question.

Next a statement which had been written down when Taylor was first detained was read out. It said: 'Chief Inspector Imber has asked me a question and I refused to answer it. I am not going to give anyone away, as I am single, and the other is a married man with five children. If I suffer he will thank me for it some day.'

This statement was, however, misleading as it had been taken after Taylor was arrested for cycle stealing and not for murder. Witnesses were then brought forward testifying to the lack of closeness between Mr and Mrs Phillips and the Taylor family, and the case was then adjourned. It was restarted the following Friday with Taylor entering the dock, 'with his usual cool air'. One important witness was Mary Jane Cotton of Rose Cottage, Stoneleigh. She had until recently lived at Stoke Park where her cottage had overlooked the back of Hawthorne Cottage. She testified that on the night of 10 January, between nine thirty and ten, she had stood at her back door with her husband and they saw a light in the conservatory. The couple noted that it was not from a lantern or a candle but was a steady light. The light they recalled, 'seemed to be like someone looking around ... because it was moving around'. On examination Mrs Cotton said, however, that she could not swear that it was a bicycle lamp.

Other witnesses told of Taylor's lack of money, ordering things he could not pay for, often claiming that he was getting married. Next Mr Johnstone of the Vernon Cycle Company was called and testified regarding the cycle, which it was claimed Taylor sold to Eales. He recalled in 1903 he had a dozen frames like that of Lamont's bicycle, but he only sold one other with back-stays like Lamont's. Asked if the japanning on the bike was done with the same brush, as that on the lamp Johnstone would not commit himself. After five hours the hearing was once again adjourned, and reopened the following day.

The press noted on the day that there was a large crowd present in St Mary's Street, which consisted mainly of women, and it was noted that they also formed a large proportion of the spectators in court. The day's evidence was mainly concerned with the identification of the cycle lamp found in the kitchen of Hawthorne Cottage, now known as the, 'Stoke Lamp'. It was noted on this day that Taylor took a very close interest in the lamp, looking at it, 'through the bars of the dock.' He also frequently smiled during the sitting at the two warders in the dock with him. But still the press noted, 'his coolness still remains unshaken'.

One of the first witnesses was John Lamont, who in 1903 lived in Walsgrave. He told the court that at the end of 1902, or the beginning of 1903, his brother had purchased a cycle with a lamp from Frank Johnstone. The brothers initially shared the machine, but it was ridden mostly by John. He swore to the court that apart from odd changes such as seat, handlebars and brake this was his cycle; the same cycle as found in Eales's workshop. He added that one evening when he was riding home from school a boy had thrown a stone at him and it had made an almost unnoticeable dent in the rim of the back wheel. He then pointed out the dent to the judges, and added that in the winter of 1904 he had fallen off the bicycle on his way to school, this resulted in a dent in the handlebar. The handle bar had however been changed, after it was stolen.

During this incident, he told the court, the lamp had fallen off although he had not noticed this until later and so the following morning he had returned to the spot and found the lamp in two pieces. He noticed that the fall had damaged the burner, as it would not wind up properly, being slightly out of shape. When he returned from school he cleaned the lamp and noticed a dent on the bottom of the lamp and on the burner and by the winder, which caused a slight leak. He knew the lamp well as he normally polished it three times a week. He also told the court that on 16 September he rode the cycle with the lamp into Coventry and left it in the *Star* Yard, Earl Street, near Mr Johnstone's cycle works. When he returned fifteen minutes later the cycle had gone.

As Lamont pointed out, the smooth tyres were those he had put on and the front wheel was wobbly. He had taken it to be tightened but was told it had been strained and would always have a slight wobble. The *Coventry Herald* reported that when he looked again at the lamp, 'The witness pointed out the various dents that he had referred to, and said that the nameplate on the lamp came off as he was cleaning it. When he lost the lamp the previous year there was no black upon it; the lamp was all bright. There were red and green lights inside, and these were clear; they were not covered up in any way.' He also stated that he used ordinary cycle lamp wick in the lamp before it was stolen. James Lamont was then called and confirmed that the cycle in court was the machine that his brother had purchased. He also identified the 'Stoke Lamp' adding that it had a loose spring.

Thomas Eales was then called and confirmed to the court that he had made the tool suspected as the murder weapon for Taylor, and that Taylor had sold him the cycle frame and the other parts, such as the wheels which had come from Taylor via another person, and that he had seen them in Taylor's workshop. He also told the court that he thought Taylor's firing of a revolver in his own workshop was done simply as a joke. When cross examined he told the court he and Taylor did a 'bit' of dealing with cycles

Taylor's state of mind and his alleged drunken condition on the day and night of the murder were the next factors to be considered. William Hanson landlord of the *Woolpack* in Spon Street was called and told the judges that he had known Taylor for about four years as he had done jobs for him. He told them that Taylor was at the inn between eight and ten, playing darts. He noted that he was very excited; seeming a little 'wild' and 'strange' in a condition he had never seen him in before. Asked if he thought Taylor was drunk, Hanson replied, 'No, I say distinctively he was not drunk.' The hearing was then adjourned until Monday morning.

The inquest was resumed and Charles Jordan of Cross Cheaping informed the court that Taylor came to him nearly half-an-hour after leaving the Woolpack and said he was, 'pretty nearly drunk.' They had supper and Taylor told him he was going to a club in Hill Street. Both Hanson and Jordan stated when asked, that on that night Taylor was wearing black clothes and a trilby hat, this became an important fact when Benjamin Taylor was called again. He had said in a previous sitting that he saw two men around 4.30 am near the cottage.

Benjamin Taylor now stated that on that brilliantly lit moonlit morning he saw that the younger of the two men was wearing black clothes and a trilby hat. He also stated that he had seen the same person at the victim's funeral, and also thought that the older man was also there. He identified the second man as Taylor's father and the sitting was adjourned.

On recommencing the inquest Inspector Imber told the court he had made enquiries and examined the prisoner's father, and on being pressed admitted that the witness was 'probably' mistaken. He then said that when the prisoner was questioned regarding the cycle, and asked if it was stolen he replied, 'It perhaps was stolen, I don't know. I sold them for a certain fellow at Foleshill. I shan't say who he is.' Inspector Imber then asked Taylor about the fact that two people had identified him as being abroad at the time of the murder, to which Taylor replied, 'Oh, yes, will that job come off in March Assizes', and when asked the name of the second man he responded, 'Leave me for a quarter or half an hour and come to me again. Imber then left him alone in the cell but returned half an hour later and asked for his response, to which Taylor replied bluntly, 'I have nothing more to tell you.'

The court was then given a detailed description of the murder scene and the wounds suffered by the victims; wounds which appeared to have been made by a long metal object with a curved end. This of course matched the missing tool that Eales had made for Taylor. Then Dr Bostock of Birmingham was examined concerning Taylor's clothes, which he had analysed for blood residue. Much to the court's surprise he stated Taylor's clothes contained no blood residues or evidence of recent cleaning. His hat was also clear, the pink staining on it being found to be dye. It was also pointed out that although the wick and paper used in the lamp was identical to that found in Eales's workshop such material could be found in most retailers throughout the country.

Taylor's mother then took the stand and told the court that on the night of the murder her son stayed out all night and she first saw him at 7 am warming his hands in the kitchen. Asking him where he had been he said he had slept in his workshop in Jenner Street, that he had broken the pledge, got drunk and was so ashamed he did not want to wake them up. She also told the court that her son had a lamp like the 'Stoke Lamp', but it was now missing, and he owned several hats including a trilby. She also stated that on that morning he was wearing a cap, and although his clothes were creased she saw no blood only a little wood dust. Then, when making a statement about her husband's presence that night, she felt faint and had to be given a chair.

When asked about the fact that she swooned when Imber showed her the lamp, she told the court that she had felt faint before Imber had mentioned it, and although her son had ridden a cycle for years she could not say for certain that the 'Stoke Lamp' was his. Then, on being re-examined, some of her evidence changed and she stated that her son was pressed for money and she could not swear the lamp was not his. She also, when pressed, admitted that although her son looked dusty she did not examine his clothes closely, as he was standing warming his hands by the fire.

The *Herald* then states that the prisoner was formally charged and, 'He bore himself firmly, though his face retained the flush that came to it upon the appearance of his mother in the witness box.' The court then adjourned and recommenced at 2.30 when the defence read a statement from Taylor, which read, 'I am not guilty. I do not wish to call any witnesses and do not propose to give evidence on my own behalf.' Mr Masser, for the defence, then addressed the court claiming that it was extremely doubtful that the murder took place on the 10th, and that investigation had shown that Taylor was not in financial trouble and actually owed less than nine pounds. He also claimed that Taylor's nature on that day, 'chucking girls under the chin and being in a larky humour,' was not the way a murderer would act. He also asked the court not to attach too much importance to the fact that Taylor gave two versions as to where he slept that night, one claiming he was in the water closet and the second at his workshop. He also pointed out that Boneham, who claimed to have seen the prisoner at Stoke Park, said he was slim when apparently he was not, and Benjamin Taylor the other witness said he wore a trilby when Boneham said he wore a cap. What he did not point out was that witnesses who saw Taylor in the evening said he wore a trilby, and yet his mother who saw him the next morning said he was then wearing a cap. Does this suggest he changed his clothes?

He also told the court to consider the fact that as the father was not charged, the witness Taylor was 'clearly' wrong. Also Charles Taylor was drunk, and yet Boneham and Taylor said the man they saw was sober. That said, the landlord of the *Woolpack* said he certainly was not. Masser also reminded the court that Taylor's clothes had no blood on them, no blood on his boots or dirt proving that he walked the footpath. Masser pointed out that these 'discrepancies' cast serious doubt on the evidence against Taylor. Masser continued:

> *As to the so-called jemmies or scrapers – they were ordered openly, not secretly. Was a man, because he could not give an account of a jemmy, and because the wounds of the old people were curved, something like the curve of a jemmy to be accused of having murdered them? Could one man kill both these people – old people attached to each other? I do not think so. The evidence showed that there were two people in the room* [this fact does not appear anywhere in the evidence], *one of whom was strong enough to knock down the woman with two blows, while the other less powerful required sixteen blows to finish the man. That being so, would the man who first killed the woman hand the weapon to the other to kill the man? I do not think so.*

Masser claimed that two men with two weapons must have committed the murder. That said, the fact that the woman was gagged might mean that she was caught in bed, while the husband was still downstairs. Then gagged and told to stay in bed. When the husband entered the room he was knocked to the ground and the women in a panic tried to flee the room and was struck down and killed. The killer may then have returned to the husband and in his self-induced frenzy struck him more times than necessary; individual strength does not come into it. Alternatively the killer may have wanted to terrorize the couple into telling him where their money was hidden. Having gagged the wife he found that the husband resisted and so struck him down, that caused the wife to panic so he then attacked and killed her. There may have been a second person but that does not mean that the second person took part in the deed.

Masser concluded by saying that the evidence concerning the cycle was weak and that as for the lamp no one could swear they had seen the prisoner with it. Although the prisoner, if he had been wiser, would not have made some of the statements he had, none of those statements amounted to an admission of guilt. He asked that Taylor should not be sent before a jury, and buttered up the judges by saying that a jury could not do more than the honourable judges had already done.

The judges then left the court and returned after ten minutes and the court clerk read out their statement that after careful consideration, the court is of the opinion that Charles Ernest Robert Taylor should be tried before a court of the assizes, and is therefore remanded to appear at Warwick County Court at the next assizes.

Taylor was returned to Warwick Gaol and meanwhile in Coventry a Coroner's Inquest started for which Taylor returned as he chose to be present during the inquiry. The wounds that had killed the victims were discussed, and the coroner asked Dr Loudon if they had been inflicted by the same 'bicep' power on both victims. Loudon replied, 'I can hardly go as far as to say so, but the same amount of force could account for all the wounds.' The coroner then added, 'It is not impossible you think that the injuries may have been inflicted by two people.' 'Not at all,' Loudon responded. 'Do you think that the same instrument or an instrument exactly similar, could have inflicted the wounds?' 'Yes, I think so,' Loudon replied.

John Boneham's evidence in which he believed he had seen Taylor on the footpath leading to the Walsgrave Road was again discussed. His evidence was called into question because he had described the man as slim. Taylor was told to stand up in court and Boneham agreed he was not slim. However, it was pointed out that the records showed that Taylor had gained 22 lbs while incarcerated. Boneham still insisted Taylor was the man he saw on the night of the murder.

Benjamin Taylor was then examined and told the court that he had seen Taylor with another man on the Binley Road, while on his way to work at Alfred Herbert's. Masser, for the prisoner, knowing that he had identified Taylor's father as the elder man told him to stand up and asked, 'Is that the man you identified as the elder man?' Taylor was more indecisive than previously and replied, 'I don't say I identified him. It is not my place to identify anyone. It is the police's place to identify anyone.' Masser responded, 'I ask you if the man standing up in court is one of the men you saw?' Taylor appearing moved at this point replied, 'You have a resemblance to the man Mr. Taylor.' Taylor's father responded by saying, 'If you say I am the man, you are a liar.' Masser persisted with the attack and asked Taylor whether or not he had told Inspector Imber that Charles Taylor's father was the man he had seen on the Binley Road and at the funeral. Taylor said he had not. When asked why he went to the funeral he told the court that the police had asked him to. The coroner then said, 'Are you going to say that the accused is the man you saw or, that he is similar to the one you saw?' 'Well he has every appearance,' said Taylor. The coroner continued, 'Are you going to say the same with regard to the elder man in court?' 'Yes,' Taylor replied.

On the following day, the inquest considered both Taylor's state of mind on the day of the murders, and also his clothes. Charles Jordan testified that the clothes shown in court were not the same as those he saw Taylor wearing on the night of the murders, and added that when he left him, Taylor was in drink, but not morose or boisterous. Dr Loudon gave evidence that he believed that despite the large amounts of blood in the room the killer would not necessarily have much blood on his clothes. The coroner then asked Dr Loudon, 'Do you believe that the clothes that have been presented today were the clothes that were used and worn by the person who committed the injuries.' Masser then intervened saying this was not evidence, to which the coroner replied he would pass it by, but would cover it in his summing up. Inspector Imber subsequently stated that he had not acquired Taylor's clothes until seventeen days after the murder.

The next day Charles Taylor's father was in the dock, and he told the court that Taylor owed him rent from the previous November and he had remonstrated with him over that and his other debts. The court was told that on 20 January he had made a statement that his son had come home about ten o'clock, and on the 22nd he changed his statement and said his son did not return home on the night of the murders. He admitted he had told a lie, then his statement was read in which he swore to Inspector Imber that he saw his son come down stairs on the morning after the murder. Masser interjected asking if it was not sufficient that he admitted he lied, but the Town Clerk replied, 'No, I want to know about lie number two.'

The coroner in summing up brought forward the clothes again saying:

The clothes spoken of on the night of the 10th were a double breasted coat and a black suit. The prisoner was seen on that night by Mr. Jordan, who described similar clothes. So far as the clothes are concerned I must tell you that you must take into consideration the time of the commitment of the murder ... the prisoner had an opportunity of at least something like 17 days to do what he liked with them.

The verdict finally came, that 'the prisoner Charles Ernest Robert Taylor did with malice aforethought kill and slay Richard Phillips and Mary Phillips'. Taylor stood with his arms tightly folded over his chest and head held high, but looking flushed while the clerk sent him to trial at the next assizes. On leaving the building the crowds again swamped St Mary's Street.

The trial moved to Warwick and Taylor pleaded not guilty to the charges laid against him. The *Coventry Herald* commented at the time that he:

looked in full flush of young manhood; certainly he seemed a credit to his sojourn of some months in Warwick Gaol. Ruddy of face, plump cheeks, broad shoulders and full frame, he was a picture of health. His hair was neatly parted and he had grown a

*light moustache since his last appearance at Coventry. He was
well dressed in a black suit ... he seemed fully at ease without
being indifferent ... Several times he smiled at points in the
evidence.*

Very little new evidence emerged, Charles Jordan manager of
Dresden's tailors confirmed again that Taylor came to visit him
on the night of the murder. He told the jury that the suit he
was wearing at that time was made by his firm and that the suit
on display in court supposed to be worn be Taylor on that
night was not the same suit.

Taylor's defence attacked the witnesses Taylor and Boneham
who had placed him near the scene of the murder and brought
forward small discrepancies in earlier evidence, concerning the
way he held his head, whether his collar showed and his size.
Boneham was asked if the man he had seen was of slim build
as he had previously stated. Boneham replied, 'He was at the
time I met him.' Counsel, 'Is he as slim now as he was then?'
Boneham, 'I don't think he is.' Counsel, 'He has put on
weight?' Boneham, 'Yes he has.' Counsel, 'Had you any doubt
whatever that this was the man you saw?' The court waited and
Boneham replied firmly, 'No!'

Taylor's mother was called to the stand and asked about the
lamp. She said when she was originally asked about it, it
reminded her of her son's lamp as it had red and green lights.
The lamp she said was kept on the tall shelf in the scullery. She
was asked if it was still there after the 11th to which she
replied, 'No, my lord.'

The trial lasted for four days and to the surprise of all, a
verdict of not guilty was reached and Taylor acquitted. The
story, however, does not end there for a short time later Taylor
was back before the court, this time for housebreaking. He was
sentenced to seven years' imprisonment: some suggested this
was a result of evidence produced during the previous case.
He was released from prison in 1914 and a few days later
appeared in the Thames Police Court charged with attempting
to commit suicide by drowning. Soon after he served in the
army and air force during the Great War. He returned to
England with his clothes stiff with blood, not his but others',

and he was taken to the Coventry and Warwickshire Hospital where he was found to be suffering from shell shock. Three months later he was transferred to Hatton Asylum, near Warwick, where he stayed for two months until his final discharge in 1917. He returned to Spencer Street where people later said he often acted, 'funny' and later moved to Northampton.

The story of Charles Ernest Robert Taylor ends at mid-day on the 7 April 1922, when John Over of Earlsdon was walking his dog along the Kenilworth Road on Gibbet Hill. He would later tell an inquest of the event:

> *I saw the deceased hanging from a tree in the wood on the right hand side of the road going towards Kenilworth. At first I thought a man was climbing the tree, but on closer investigation found that he was hanging from a branch by a piece of rope. The branch was 18 foot from the ground, and the deceased feet were four foot from the ground. I cut the body down, and saw no signs of life.*

Inspector Hawkes of Kenilworth later searched the body and found several cards on one of which was written, 'God bless my dear wife.' At the inquest held in the parlour of Gibbet Hill Farm, Taylor's father told the jury that he had last seen his son on 5 April, and although he was in good health, his spirit was broken. The coroner suggested that Taylor had been depressed and this was agreed. Taylor's daughter had written to her grandfather to tell him of her father's deep depression. This caused him to visit his son at Northampton to try to cheer him up.

He informed the inquest that that Wednesday was the last time he had seen him alive and his last words were, 'Well Dad, if I get squared up all right before Easter, I shall cycle over and see you and mother.' On the Friday evening at about 8.30 pm he heard a noise coming from the letterbox. Originally thinking children were playing a game he ignored it but later found the basket full. He took the items out which included a light, a pair of wet khaki gloves, a white rag wrapped around a pocket watch and chain, and another rag holding 1s. 8½d. The couple immediately recognized their son's watch, then found a business card which had on its back written in pencil, 'Friday night. Dear mother and father, – Cheer up and forgive me. Don't forget my poor Maggie. Love to all. Yours C. E. R. Taylor. XXXX.'

Taylor's father found his bike standing against the kitchen window and later informed the police of his concerns and waited all night for news. Taylor's wife told the inquest that he had been out of work a few weeks and was short of money, but the coroner pointed out that many others had been unemployed for far longer and it was nothing that could not be quickly remedied. It was also suggested that Taylor had no large debts, to which Mrs Taylor gave no positive answer. She told the inquest she had last seen her husband on Friday when he left on his bike saying he would not be long. However, when he did not return she informed the police. She also pointed out to the jury her surprise at her husband's death, telling the inquest that when he read of such events in the newspapers he was always adamant that he could not do such a thing himself. The inquest gave a verdict of suicide while suffering from temporary insanity and Charles Taylor, the Stoke Park murders and the Gibbet Hill suicide slipped into the mists of history.

Whether Taylor was the Stoke Park murderer we will never know for certain, but were his last moments a clue? He left his bike by the kitchen window, reflecting the place from which the murderer entered Hawthorne Cottage and through his parents door he chose to place a light, a pair of gloves, a pocket watch and a small amount of cash. Significantly in the Stoke Murder Case there was a light, the 'Stoke Lamp,' the gloves may represent the fact that no fingerprints where left or found in the cottage, a pocket watch reflecting the fact that a pocket watch was known to have been taken and 1s. 8^{1}/$_{2}d$., could this possibly have been the amount of cash, which was originally in the rifled cash box found at Hawthorne Cottage. Was his suicide his confession? We may never know for the truth died with Charles Taylor on Gibbet Hill, a place significantly noted for the execution of murderers.

Selected Sources

A Journal of the Proceedings of J. Hewitt, senior alderman of the City of Coventry and one of his Majesty's justices of the peace for the said city and county, in his duty as a Magistrate, during a period of thirty years and upwards, in cases of riots, coiners, murder, highway robberies, burglaries, returned transports and other matters. Second Edition 1790

Andrews Cuttings, Coventry Local Studies
Book of Martyrs, John Foxe
Coventry Annals (various)
Coventry Evening Telegraph
Early Records of Medieval Coventry, P Coss, 1986
Execution Broadsides
'Gesta Stephani', The Deeds of Stephen
Humorous Reminiscences of Coventry Life, T W Whitley, 1888
Justice Rolls of Eyre
Midland Daily Telegraph
Rolls of the Warwickshire and Coventry Sessions of Peace. 1377–1397, Dugdale Society
Swing 'em Fair: Coventry's Darker Side, David McGrory
The Paston Letters
The Pistol, the Knife and the Poisonous Drug or Farquar, Thompson and Beamish, booklet published 1862
The Coventry Herald
The Coventry Herald and Free Press
The Coventry Leet Book, 1907–13, Mary Dormer Harris
The Coventry Herald and Free Press and Midland Express
The Coventry Mercury
The Coventry Standard

Index